WHEN.

A Family Book of Knowledge

Octopus
Octopus Books

j032

78 940

ABOUT THIS BOOK

Life consists of asking questions. We start from the moment we learn to string words together and most of us go on asking them for the rest of our lives. Alas, we don't always find the answers. This book (and its companion volumes in this series) presents a random array of questions most commonly asked—and not only by children.

When a question springs to mind, ferreting out the answer can be a difficult business. Often the answer lies buried in a mass of information we don't need.

These books go straight to the heart of the matter and answer simple (and not so simple) questions in a down-to-earth manner.

When does the tuatara hunt? When was Washington DC made the capital of the United States? When do people stop growing?

When was Stonehenge built?

The questions are divided into six main categories. There is no attempt

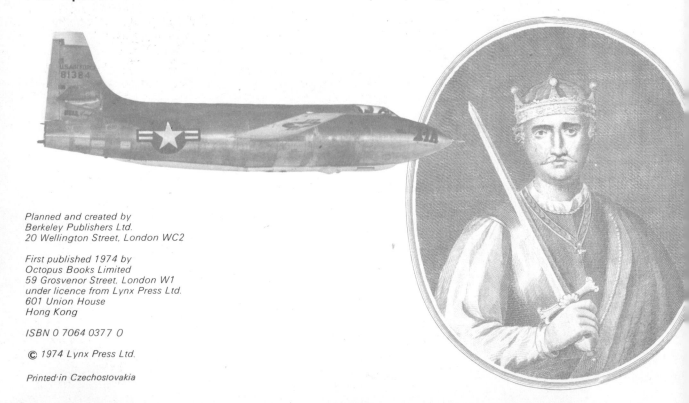

Planned and created by
Berkeley Publishers Ltd.
20 Wellington Street, London WC2

First published 1974 by
Octopus Books Limited
59 Grosvenor Street, London W1
under licence from Lynx Press Ltd.
601 Union House
Hong Kong

ISBN 0 7064 0377 0

be definitive, for millions of questions could be posed. With the help of a team of teachers and students, we've picked out the ones most commonly asked—and some that simply appeal to us.

If you know when male sticklebacks turn red and can instantly explain when a snake will dance then go to the top of the question class. If you can't, then welcome aboard. Our family book of questions will be your perfect guide and companion. If you can't find the answer to your own particular question in WHEN, well then, try WHERE or WHY or WHAT And when you've exhausted *our* questions, try dreaming up some of your own—and find out the answers for yourself!

IN THIS BOOK

Natural History

People and Events

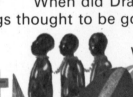

The Body and Medicine

Geography and the Earth

Science and Technology

General Knowledge

Natural History

MALE STICKLEBACK

The male stickleback's belly turns red at the start of the breeding season in spring. Normally the belly of this small fish is silver-coloured, the rest of it varying from brown to green. But when the time comes for him to mate he becomes very active in attracting females with his bright new colour.

In building the home and rearing the family the male stickleback performs many of the functions usually associated with a female fish. He chooses the place for the nest, collects the stems of various aquatic plants and binds them together using a threadlike web secreted from his kidney.

Once the female has been enticed into his nest, she will lay her eggs and depart, leaving him on guard. He watches over the eggs with great care and even looks after the baby fish.

MIGRATION

Millions of birds of many different varieties migrate at the end of summer. With unfailing regularity they leave the regions where they were born to fly to warmer climates for the winter. The following spring they return to their breeding grounds.

Each year these migratory birds travel as much as 20,000 miles, finding their way back on time with extraordinary precision. Some travel as individuals.

Migration is triggered off by the length of daylight, which apparently affects the birds' nervous systems. When the days get shorter the birds receive the signal to leave for their warmer winter grounds, and, when the daylight increases to a certain level, they receive another signal to return home.

The swallows pictured above are European swallows wintering in Africa.

nigrate? **WHEN** does a chameleon change colour?

CHAMELEON

A chameleon will change colour when it senses danger. This re- markable member of the lizard family can change colour to match its background or, at least, to become almost unrecognizable.

The ranges of colours and pat- terns of the various species differ widely, but most chameleons can become yellow or cream, green or dark brown. They can also adapt spots either dark or light depend- ing on the colour of the ground.

Apart from its response to danger, the chameleon will change colour according to the light and temperature. This mechanism is controlled from the nervous system and involves the dispersion or concentration of colour pigments in the creature's skin.

WHEN does a tree stop growing? WHEN does a cow star

TREE GROWTH

A tree never permanently stops growing as long as it lives. But in most countries each year's growth is ended during the cold and dry seasons. The annual period of growth depends on the climate. In moist tropical regions a tree may grow continuously.

Every period of growth is marked by an annual ring. This ring takes the form of a new layer of wood added to the width of the tree. So the age of a tree may be calculated. Some trees, notably the Redwood trees of California, are said to live for 4,000 years.

COW'S MILK

A cow starts to give milk between the ages of two and two-and-a-half years, after the birth of its first calf. For the first few days the milk is unfit for human consumption and is fed to the calf which is afterwards reared separately. During the milking or lactation period that follows the cow's yield usually reaches a maximum after four to six weeks and continues in decreasing quantities for nine to ten months.

To ensure a steady supply of milk, farmers arrange for their cows to calve every 12 months.

Attention to breeding has led to steady improvements in yields. A good cow may produce up to 2,000 gallons guring the lactation period.

Cows are normally milked twice a day, morning and evening. Except for the smallest herds, milking in advanced countries is usually done by machines which suck the milk from the cows' udders and transfer it to covered containers. But there are still many countries where milking is largely done by hand, in the traditional way.

WORM

If the earthworm detects an unfamiliar object next to its skin, the muscles will contract immediately and the body will turn to avoid the object. The worm will also turn in response to heat and, in a lesser degree, to light and sound.

Even the heat given out by an ordinary match some inches away, will cause a worm to retreat. Sound waves will also lead the earthworm to change direction rather than approach what, to human ears, may seem only a slight noise. Light, on the other hand, usually attracts the worm. It turns inquisitively to inspect the brighter patch, even although, of course, earthworms can live underground for long periods.

The phrase "even a worm will turn" is used in the sense that even the humblest of creatures will eventually rebel if goaded or pushed too hard. But the phrase has no real relationship to the activities of worms as such.

give milk? **WHEN** does a worm turn?

WHEN were breakfast cereals first used?

BREAKFAST CEREALS

Cereals, of course, in the general sense, including wheat, rice, maize (known as corn in Canada and the United States), rye, oats and barley were among the earliest plants grown by man. But packaged or processed cereals are a modern development.

Breakfast cereals owe their origin to the vegetarians of the last century and health fanatics who believed they could save souls by preaching the virtues of a non-meat diet.

Granula, which was the beginning of Grape-Nuts, was launched in 1863 by a man called James C. Jackson, of Danville, New York. Henry D. Perkey brought out Shredded Wheat in 1893 and Puffed Wheat was developed by Alexander Anderson in 1902.

The religious sect, the Seventh Day Adventists, made Battle Creek, Michigan, the cereal headquarters of the world when the sect formed the Western Health Reform Institute at Battle Creek in 1866, later called the Battle Creek Sanatorium. John Harvey Kellogg, who was a doctor and a writer, took over control of the Sanatorium in 1876 and his advocacy of cereals helped to develop what was to become a vast new food industry. His brother, W. K. Kellogg, started a cereal producing company in 1906.

C. W. Post was another cereal pioneer and his Postum Cereal Company formed in 1897 later developed into General Foods Corporation.

The basic idea behind packaged cereals has remained largely unchanged.

ve: Barley. Below: *Rice growing in Japan.*

WHEN does a caterpillar become a butterfly?   WHEN do

BUTTERFLY

A caterpillar starts to become a butterfly as soon as it enters the chrysalis stage, by wrapping itself in a cocoon. During this phase, known as pupation, the insect gradually develops all the butterfly characteristics, including wings. For some butterflies the transformation may be complete in one or two weeks. But others need many months before they are ready to leave the cocoon and fly away.

From the time it is hatched to the time it starts the pupation stage, a caterpillar or larva does little more than eat, grow larger and moult several times. This larval stage varies according to the species. Small caterpillars will complete their development in a week, but some large varieties will take up to two years or more.

When this period is over the caterpillar spins a cocoon under a leaf or even underground, and enters it to begin the transformation. Many cocoons are of silk.

llution kill a river?

YING RIVER

river will die when pollution aches such a level that all the vailable oxygen is absorbed.

This can happen if the oxygen used up by the presence in the ater of an excessive number of aste organisms.

Large amounts of nitrogen or hosphorus make a river's oxyen-producing plants grow so pidly that they become overrowded and die of exhaustion. hen the fish also die because they re deprived of plant food. Finally arious forms of bacteria decay nd the water becomes putrefied.

All human industrial waste produces pollution. Excessive quantities of chemicals and minerals deposited in rivers will kill the water by destroying its oxygen content.

Some rivers flowing through industrial areas have been so changed that it is possible to set fire to them. This happened to the Cuyahoga River in Ohio in 1969.

Above: *dead fish in a stagnant pond.*
Below: *detergent foam covers the surface of a river in Pennsylvania, U.S.A. The foam will gradually kill the river.*

WHEN will sharks attack a human being ? WHEN does app

SHARKS

Some sharks may attack human beings if attracted by underwater noises, erratic swimming, the presence of a large number of bathers, or the glint of jewellery or some other article. But probably the greatest provocation to a shark is the presence of blood, for instance from a speared fish or live bait.

Sharks are most likely to attack during the daytime, the areas of greatest danger being those where the sea temperature is between 16°

and 21° Centigrade (60° and 70° Fahrenheit). Most attacks seem to occur about 200 to 300 feet from the shore where the water is shallow—or no more than two or three feet in depth.

Among the kinds of sharks known to attack human beings are the tiger and the blue and grey nurse sharks. The most feared and the largest of all the shark family is the great white shark, a powerful and aggressive creature.

APPLE SCAB

Apple scab occurs when an apple tree falls victim to a fungus called *Venturia Inaequalis*, a malignant growth which slowly eats away at the leaves and fruit.

It is a widespread and serious disease affecting apple trees all over the world, but is more powerful in warm climates.

Farmers control the fungus by spraying the trees with sulphur. That is one reason why apples should be washed before eating.

scab occur? **WHEN** does a snake "dance"?

WHEN do animals become mutants?

MUTANTS

Animals are said to be mutants when they show characteristics different from the rest of their species. Mutations are processes by which the hereditary properties of some of the reproductive cells in animals are altered.

In nature these changes can take place spontaneously and unpredictably. But they are rare, and little is known about this cause, beyond the fact that the longer an animal takes to breed, the less likely it is to give birth to a mutant.

Nowadays, the most common causes of animals producing mutants are chemical substances and radiation. Indeed, radiation is a rapidly increasing hazard.

Animals born from parents who have suffered the effects of more than normal radiation are invariably mutants. Cows have been known to grow a fifth leg. In the Pacific Islands, where nuclear tests have been conducted, there are fish which have forgotten how to swim and have been found on land. Birds have lost the power to fly, and some may have only one wing. Turtle mutants are unable to find the sea and consequently die.

Animal mutants have long intrigued and frightened people. In Greek mythology, mutants such as dogs and horses with two heads were believed to possess magical powers.

SNAKE'S "DANCE"

There are two occasions when a snake will "dance"—both connected with the mating season. In the first case the dancing partners are both male and their performance appears to be a form of aggression designed to impress the female.

The second occasion is a nuptial dance between male and female. First the snakes pursue each other and coil together. Then the couple raise their necks and heads as if forming the shape of the letter U. During the dance, which may last an hour, the male rubs its chin against the female's neck.

The nuptial dance occurs mainly among European snakes, but the males' dance of aggression is to be seen all over the world especially among rattlesnakes, adders and cobras.

WHEN does a tadpole become a frog?
WHEN were the American bison almost wipe

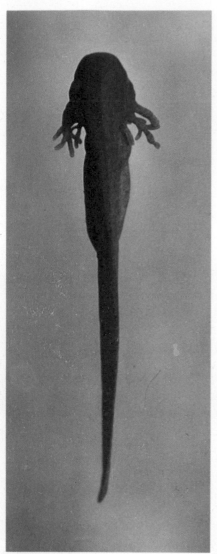

TADPOLES

Frogs' eggs become tadpoles within two weeks of being laid in the water, but tadpoles may take anything from two months to three years to change completely into frogs.

The time taken seems to depend on the environment. Tadpoles will generally develop faster in warmer waters. Also the more advanced species of frog have simplified and shortened the process of transformation.

Tadpoles, like fish, breathe through gills. They develop lungs during the change-over, gain legs and lose their tails. The menu changes, too—from plants to very small insects.

AMERICAN BISON

The American bison were near to extinction by 1900, although they numbered more than 60 million when the white man first arrived in their feeding grounds.

Buffalo, as the bison were commonly called, were the prime essential of the Plains Indian's economy. The powerful animal's meat, bones, and hide provided the Indians with food, medicine, clothing and shelter.

At first the white man, too, killed the buffalo for meat and hides. But after 1850, as the American–Indian war neared its climax, United States soldiers began to slaughter the animals indiscriminately to force the Indians to leave their homelands. With the advent of the railroad the killing of the bison became a sport. Travellers would shoot from railroad carriages, leaving the carcases to rot by the tracks. In less than 50 years about 50 million buffalo had been exterminated.

The voices of those who wished to save the animal from extinction were heeded just in time. From the few survivors, new herds were reared. Today buffalo are increasing in numbers, with herds totalling several thousand.

TUATARA

The tuatara is the only survivor of the beak-headed order of reptiles, called Rhynchocephalia, that goes back to the time of the dinosaurs. It hunts by night and its prey are insects. Like the coelecanth, a prehistoric fish that still survives, the tuatara is almost a living fossil.

It can now be found only on some of the small islets off the coast of New Zealand, having been exterminated from the mainland. It basks in the sun during the day and burrows into the soil for safety. It is covered in scales and grows to about 30 ins.

ut ? **WHEN** does the Tuatara hunt ?

8

WHEN does a tree have to be pruned? WHEN was tea firs

PRUNING

Trees have to be pruned to protect their health, improve their appearance or remove danger to people or property. Sometimes it is necessary to remove broken, dead or diseased branches, to restore vigour to an ageing tree by cutting back and to admit more air and light by thinning out the centre.

One of the most obvious reasons for pruning trees is to control their growth within the space available for them to flourish. In this type of pruning, live-pruning as it is called, branches are lopped from the trees to control their size and to maintain a pleasing shape.

Sometimes trees are "topped" by removing some of the upper trunk. Pollard pruning involves cutting the trees back to a point at which strong branches are to be allowed to grow. As shoots grow from these points they are cut back each year. This method makes a very ugly tree shape. The lightest method of pruning is known as drop-crotching, which trims only the upper and outer branches.

Another type of pruning is orchard pruning, for stimulating the production of flowers and fruit on fruit trees. Here the farmer tries to maintain a framework of branches which will best allow the sunlight to penetrate to the middle of the tree's crown.

Most deciduous trees may be pruned at any time of the year. The pruning of evergreen trees with needle-like leaves should normally be limited to the removal of dead wood.

Dead-pruning, or brashing, is the cutting away of dead or dying side branches, most often used with conifers growing in plantations.

The last type of pruning is side-shoot pruning or shrouding, which means the removal of small side branches on such trees as pollards or limes to provide a knot-free

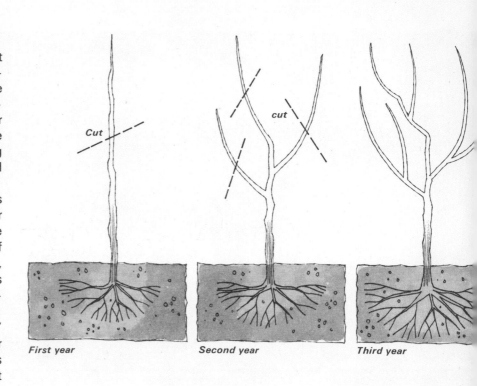

First year   Second year   Third year

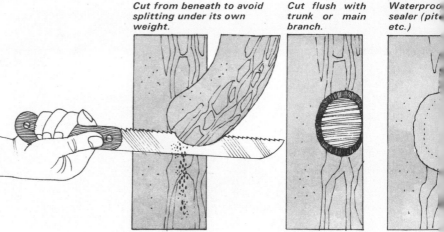

Cut from beneath to avoid splitting under its own weight.

Cut flush with trunk or main branch.

Waterproof sealer (pitch etc.)

In pruning, leave a lateral A growing right at the base of the fruiting shoot. Leave second shoot B and third shoot C. The idea is that A will produce next year's flower bud, B is retained to produce leaves and C will pull the sap upwards as the weeks proceed. B and C cut back in the middle of July about half-way down. A is not touched but if sub-laterals grow out at points D then these must be pinched out in July. In winter the fruited branch is cut at F.

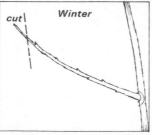

Winter   Spring   Summer

bottom length of timber.

Pruning means causing wounds and these may cause disease. Special dressings available at most

garden supply stores should be applied to cuts more than an inch in diameter to protect the trees from fungi.

TEA

We do not know when the tea plant was first cultivated, but the earliest mention of it occurs in a Chinese dictionary, the *Erh Ya*, about the year 350.

The cultivation of tea is believed to have begun in the province of Szechwan in central China. From there its cultivation and use as a beverage spread throughout China and Japan under the patronage of Buddhist priests. Perhaps it was this religious connection which gave rise to the Japanese legend about the discovery of tea. According to this story, tea first grew in China at a spot where the Buddhist saint Bodhidharma, who is said to have spent nine years in meditation before a wall, once fell asleep. He was said to have been so annoyed with himself when he awoke that he cut off his eyelids and threw them on the ground, where they took root and grew into a tea plant.

Tea was brought to Europe by the Dutch via Java in 1610 and became increasingly fashionable from the middle of the 17th Century. In England tea (pronounced tay) eventually began to oust coffee with the encourage-ment of the British East India Company who enjoyed a tea trade monopoly. India's tea industry was founded in 1834 after Major Robert Bruce had found the plant growing in the north.

While Britain began to change from coffee to tea, America did the reverse after the Boston Tea Party of 1773 when the East India Company's tea was thrown into the harbour as a protest against British taxation.

Tea is drunk by about half the world's population, but is second to coffee in commercial importance.

PLANTS

Plants breathe oxygen and carbon dioxide. In daylight they produce their own food at the same time by a process known as photosynthesis. During this process the plants release more oxygen into the atmosphere than they breathe in.

The effect of the plants' feeding and breathing system is that they exhale oxygen during the day and carbon dioxide during the night. This is the reason for the old custom in hospitals of removing plants and flowers from the wards at night and bringing them back in the morning. Without enough plants, the world's atmosphere would not be replenished with sufficient oxygen for the human race to survive.

Generally plants breathe more slowly the colder it becomes. Some plants, including many trees, go into a form of hibernation during the winter, with their breathing reduced to a minimum.

CATS IN SEASON

A female cat can be in season five times a year. It is only during these periods, which last about five days each, that the cat is fertile. Her mating call is a shrill caterwauling.

The domestic cat, as a rule, goes in season for the first time between the ages of seven and twelve months. Her pregnancy generally lasts two months. A few hours before she delivers her litter she stops eating. A normal litter of kittens is four.

WHEN does a hermit crab change its shell? WHEN do bee

HERMIT CRAB

A hermit crab changes its shell when it has grown large enough to need a bigger home. This type of crab has a soft abdomen or "tail", which is folded up under the body, but it is not protected by a shell of its own as are most other crabs. Instead, the hermit uses empty snail shells as portable shelters, often having to fight with another crab for possession of an attractive home. Sometimes the homeseeker pulls out the original occupier, eats it and then takes over the shell.

One of the claws of the hermit is larger than the other. The crab uses this to stop up the entrance after withdrawing into the shell. The last two legs on its abdomen have roughened pads which grip the inside of the shell and hold the body in position. The crab has a spiral-shaped abdomen and moves in and out of its shell with a spiral movement.

One kind of hermit occupies a sponge which conveniently grows at the same pace as the crab. Sometimes sea-anemones enter into partnership with hermit crabs and take up residence on top of the shells. The crab provides the sea-anemone with transport and in return, receives an extra shield against attack.

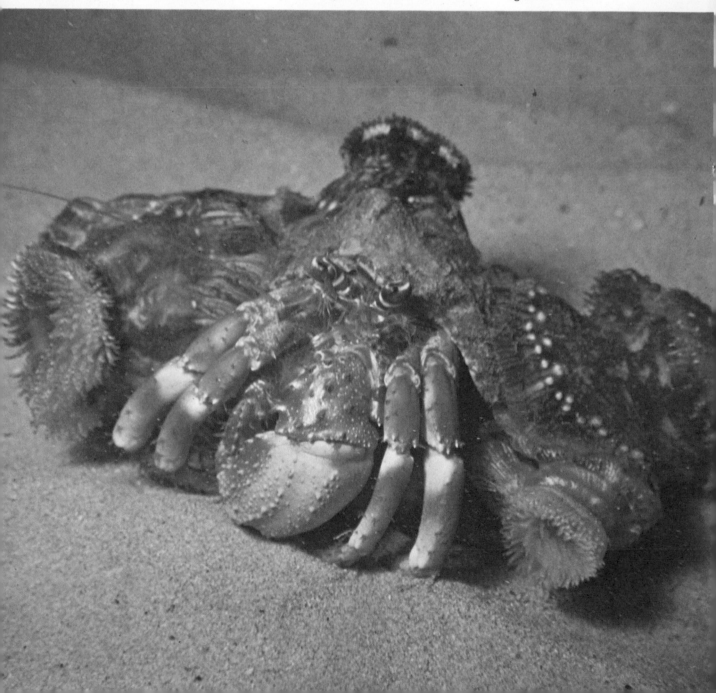

warm? **WHEN** did the pterodactyl live?

BEES SWARM

Bees swarm in late spring in search of a new home. During the winter the queen bee begins to lay her eggs and the colony sets about rearing its young. As the weather becomes warmer and the early flowers appear, the raising of young bees increases rapidly.

By the end of spring the colony has become so overcrowded that a large number of the bees, including the old queen, leave the hive and establish a new colony. In the old colony a new queen emerges who will experience the same swarming instincts the following year. And so the cycle of activity goes on.

PTERODACTYL

Pterodactyls (or pterosaurs) lived between 150 million and 70 million years ago. These extraordinary reptiles were able to fly. Some had a wing-span of over 25 feet, making them by far the largest flying animals known to man. Their skulls were often longer than four feet.

Unlike the birds, their descendants, pterodactyls must have been unable to perch upright. They probably hung upside down like bats when sleeping or at rest.

Since most remains of pterodactyls have been discovered among marine sediments, it seems likely that these flying dinosaurs found their food in the sea, like seagulls, by diving for fish.

WHEN does a lizard shed its tail? WHEN does a drone die?

LIZARD'S TAIL

A lizard is capable of shedding its tail at any time. If a lizard is attacked it may sacrifice its tail in an attempt to surprise and confuse the enemy.

When a lizard's tail is caught by an assailant or a trap, it will simply snap off and enable the reptile to escape.

Although some lizards' tails can be four times as long as the rest of their bodies, the loss is only temporary. A new tail can be grown quickly from the old stump.

RUBBER

Although the remarkable properties of the rubber tree were known to the Aztecs and other South American Indians, for perhaps a thousand years, rubber was unknown in Europe until the discovery of the New World.

Pietro Martyre d'Anghiera, chaplain to the court of Ferdinand of Aragon, Castile and Léon, gave the first written account of the elastic gum in his book *De Orbo Novo*. In it he described a game played by Aztec children using rubber balls. He was particularly amazed by the balls' ability to bounce back into the air after being thrown to the ground.

In 1615, about 100 years later, another Spaniard, Juan de Torquemada, described how the Indians made incisions into rubber trees and collected the milk or sap which oozed out. When dried, this rubber milk was used for making bottles and soles for footwear.

Workers and drone on honeycomb. The drone has the bigger eyes.

DRONE

The male bee, or drone, dies when there is no more nectar available from the fields. The reason for this is that, when the worker bees can no longer collect nectar for the hive, the production of honey stops. Deprived of their food the drones rapidly grow weak and are carried from the hive by the workers to die.

The drone takes 24 days to develop from the egg to a fully grown male and may live as an adult for several months. Its only function in the bee's community is as a potential mate for the queen.

LAND ANIMALS

Animals first appeared on earth about 430 million years ago, but did not begin to resemble the ones we know today until 360 million years later. Sharks, however, were already abundant about 340 million years ago.

It seems that the first land animals were insects such as scorpions and millipedes. But they were greatly different from today's insects. Next to develop were reptiles, the ancestors of lizards and crocodiles.

About 180 million years ago the first mammals began to develop on land along with primitive birds. During this period the forerunners of apes began to appear. The earliest species lived both on the land and in the water. It took about 20 million years for animals to develop the art of breathing air and so to live on land.

WHEN was rubber discovered?

WHEN were the first land animals?

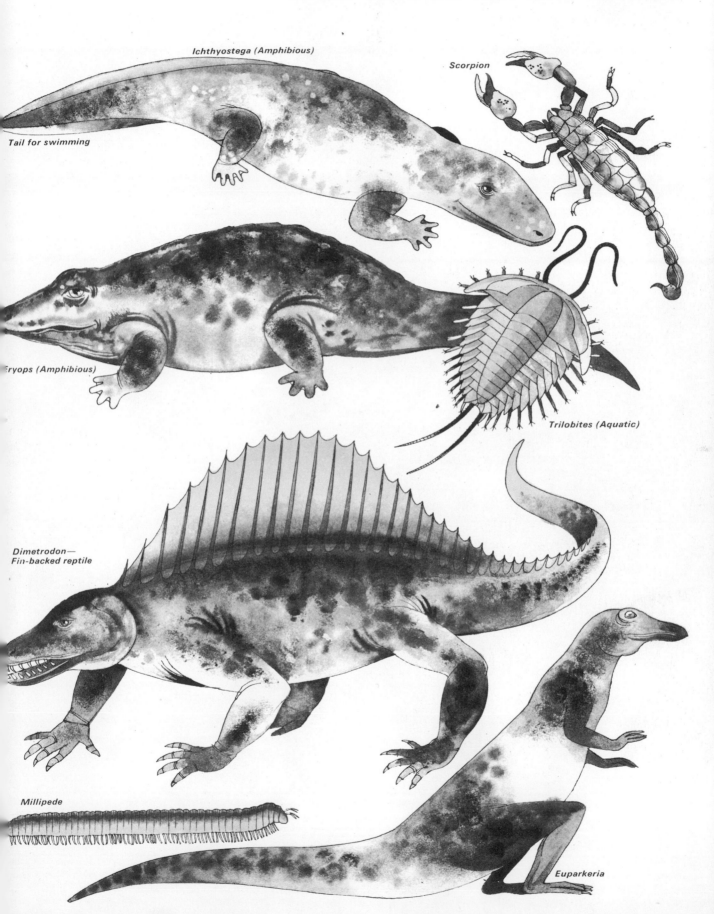

Ichthyostega (Amphibious)

Tail for swimming

Scorpion

Eryops (Amphibious)

Trilobites (Aquatic)

Dimetrodon—
Fin-backed reptile

Millipede

Euparkeria

WHEN do stags fight ? WHEN does a forest become petrified

WHEN do snakes shed their skins?

STAGS

Stags, the red deer of Europe, fight in autumn and winter for possession of the females or does. Most stags are polygamous and collect harems. A stag wishing to add to its harem at the expense of another's will challenge its rival to a duel.

At other times stags are prone to solitary wandering. But when the breeding season arrives, their fighting instincts are aroused. Occasionally the stags' antlers become so firmly interlocked in combat that they cannot free themselves. In such cases the battle ends with the deaths of both contestants from starvation.

SNAKE SKINS

Snakes shed their skins when they outgrow them. This happens continually, because snakes keep growing throughout their lives, although more slowly as they get older.

The skins are discarded at regular intervals of one to three months, according to the variety of snake. During this process, which is known as sloughing, the old skin is turned back on itself, beginning at the lips and gradually revealing the new skin underneath. When sloughing has ended, the old skin will have been turned completely inside out and left in one piece.

PETRIFIED FOREST

A forest becomes petrified or turned to stone under certain conditions, through the action over the centuries of water containing large quantities of minerals.

Tree trunks buried ages ago under mud, sand or volcanic ash have been gradually transformed as water seeped into the empty cells of the decaying wood, filling them with mineral matter and preserving every detail of the original structure.

Petrified forests have been found in many parts of North and South America, dating from different geological periods and containing stone replicas of the trees that grew in those eras. The most famous of these forests is the Petrified Forest National Park in north Arizona, in the United States. There thousands of stone trunks and logs have been exposed to view through the rain washing away the soil in which they were buried. Although now composed of a mineral called silica, the original details of the trees can be studied through a microscope. Some of the trunks are up to 80 feet long and three to four feet in diameter. They are the fossils of cone-bearing trees belonging to Triassic times, the age of the dinosaurs, and are more than 150 million years old.

People and Events

AKBAR'S EMPIRE

Jalal-ud-Din Mohammed Akbar (1542–1605), the greatest of the Mogul emperors of India, was a ruler only in name when he came to the throne in 1556. His Mongolian grandfather, Baber, had established a Mohammedan empire in northern India through a combination of daring, luck and military skill. But his father had been driven from the capital, Delhi, by a usurper.

With able generalship, Akbar overthrew all his rivals and embarked upon a career of conquest which, by 1562, gave him domain over the Punjab and Multan, the basin of the Ganges and Jumna Rivers, Gwalior to the south and Kabul in Afghanistan in the northwest. Subsequently he crossed the Narbada River into the Deccan and extended his dominion southward. By 1605, his empire contained 15 provinces, or *subahs*, and stretched from the Hindu Kush mountains to the Godocari River and from Bengal to Gujarat.

He was not only a great general, but also a great statesman. He established an excellent administrative system and came to be on friendly terms with the former Hindu rulers, respecting their religion and marrying two of their princesses. Under his rule, art and literature flourished, while scholars

from all over the world were invited to court and encouraged to discuss with Akbar all aspects of philosophy and religion.

After 1582 he formed a religious sect with himself as spiritual leader, but did not force his subjects to become members. He died at Agra on October 16, 1605, and is remembered as a wise, sincere and generous leader.

UNITED KINGDOM

The United Kingdom was formed in 1801 when an Act of Union brought Ireland under the same parliament with England, Scotland and Wales. The official name of the country was changed to the United Kingdom of Great Britain and Ireland. But 26 Irish counties left the Union in 1922 and formed the Irish Free State, now the Republic of Ireland. Five years later the Royal and Parliamentary Titles Act named the union as the United Kingdom of Great Britain and Northern Ireland.

Wales was the first to unite with England, having been subdued by King Edward I in 1282. The heir to the English throne has been known as the Prince of Wales ever since Edward gave the title to his baby son in 1301. But it was not until 1536 when Henry VIII, a Tudor monarch of Welsh descent, was on the throne, that an Act of Union peacefully incorporated the Principality into the kingdom.

The name Great Britain came into use after James VI of Scotland succeeded to the English throne in 1603 as James I and united the two crowns, though not the nations. Another Act of Union brought England and Scotland under one government in 1707.

The Union flag of the present kingdom is composed of the flag of England (white with an upright red cross), the flag of Scotland (blue with a diagonal white cross) and the red diagonal cross of Ireland.

On May 29, 1953, under the Royal Titles Act, a proclamation was issued which gave the Queen the title: Elizabeth the Second, by the Grace of God, of the United Kingdom of Great Britain and Northern Ireland and of her other Realms and Territories Queen, Head of the Commonwealth, Defender of the Faith.

ormed? **WHEN** was the Battle of Hastings?

WHEN did Drake sail round the world?

BATTLE OF HASTINGS

The Battle of Hastings was fought on October 14, 1066, on a ridge 10 miles north-west of Hastings in Sussex, England.

The events which led to the battle began when William, Duke of Normandy, in France, extracted a promise from Harold, chief minister of the Saxon king Edward the Confessor, that he would support the Norman's succession to the English throne. When Edward died on January 5, 1066, and Harold was chosen king by an assembly of nobles and citizens, William decided to seize what he claimed was his by right.

In September, while the Normans were still waiting for the wind to change to carry them across the English Channel, Harold had to march northwards into Yorkshire to repulse an invasion led by Harald Hardrada, the seven-foot king of Norway.

The Saxons crushed the invaders in a desperate battle at Stamford Bridge, but Harold was still in York when he received the news that William's army had landed near Hastings. He instantly hurried south, mobilized a new, largely untrained, army of about 7,000 men and led them against the Normans 5,000 strong.

During the battle Harold defended a piece of high ground protected by a barricade. At first the two-handed Saxon battle axes beat back the Norman attacks. But William triumphed with cunning generalship, luring the Saxons from their strong positions by pretended retreats and ordering his archers to aim high in the air so that their arrows fell on heads unprotected by the wall of shields. A chance arrow killed Harold and, as darkness fell, the English survivors scattered.

On December 25 William the Conqueror was crowned king of England in London.

William the Conqueror.

DRAKE

Francis Drake became the first Englishman to sail round the world in a voyage which lasted from 1577 to 1580. He left Plymouth on December 13 with his flagship the 100-ton Pelican, four other ships and 160 men on an expedition to the Pacific.

After sailing down the coast of South America, Drake passed through the Strait of Magellan. Then he encountered a fierce storm which drove him southward to Tierra del Fuego at the tip of the continent.

Drake's other ships had by now been lost or returned home. But the Pelican, renamed the Golden Hind, pushed on alone up the coasts of Chile and Peru, attacking towns Band plundering Spanish vessels, notably the treasure-ship Cacafuego.

After continuing northwards and claiming the Californian coast in the name of Queen Elizabeth, he decided to avoid the outraged Spaniards by sailing home across the Pacific. On reaching the Moluccas or Spice Islands, he loaded six tons of cloves, but had to throw most of the cargo overboard when the ship struck a reef.

The rest of the voyage across the Indian Ocean and round the Cape of Good Hope was comparatively uneventful, and the Golden Hind returned to Plymouth on September 26, 1580, with treasure worth £500,000. The Queen knighted Drake aboard his ship at Deptford in the Thames.

Sir Francis later became an admiral and helped to defeat the Spanish Armada in 1588. He died at sea on January 27, 1596.

WHEN were kings thought to be gods? WHEN was th

KINGS AS GODS

Throughout history, kings have often been supposed to enjoy a special relationship with the gods of their people, and in many cases, have been regarded as gods themselves.

In ancient Egypt, the king or pharaoh was believed to be divine and the Hittite kings were deified after their deaths. The Minoan kings of Crete were identified with the bull-headed sun god. In many primitive tribes in Asia and Africa, the king was identified with the sacred and divine animal of his tribe. The Swedes and Prussians of pagan Europe had divine kings, and the rulers of the Aztecs in Mexico and the Incas in Peru were, if not gods themselves, considered to be direct descendants.

Alexander the Great (356–323 B.C.), who had himself declared a god in the last year of his life, was followed by a number of god-kings throughout the Near East. In the Roman Empire the practice of making the emperor a god originated when Julius Caesar was pronounced *divus Julius* after his death. The Byzantine emperors were venerated as God's representative on earth.

The Japanese emperor was thought of as supernatural in some degree, but their term "kami", usually translated as "god", does not have such an all-embracing meaning as in the West. In China kings interceded with the gods for their people.

The statue of Amenophis II of Egypt, at Karnak. His wife is at his feet.

GUNPOWDER PLOT

"Remember, remember the fifth of November, gunpowder, treason and plot"—so goes the old English chant associated with the yearly burning on thousands of village greens and in millions of private gardens throughout England every fifth of November of the effigy of Guy Fawkes. For November 5th celebrates the discovery of the famous plot to blow up the English House of Commons.

Guy Fawkes was a Catholic gentleman who played a major role in Robert Catesby's plot to blow up King James I and his Parliament for failing to honour James's pledge to extend more toleration to the Catholics.

Catesby apparently had vague ideas of a Catholic take-over of the country.

There were five main conspirators, including Fawkes. In May 1604 they rented a house near the Parliament building and started to dig a passage which was designed to reach a point just below the House of Lords.

But in 1605 the conspirators were able to rent a neighbouring cellar which was directly beneath the Palace of Westminster. They linked their passageway to this cellar and Fawkes was allotted the task of preparing the explosion. He gathered together at least twenty barrels of gunpowder in the cellar and covered them up with wood and coal.

All seemed set for the great day, which was the November opening of Parliament. By this time the number of conspirators had risen to thirteen, one of whom, Francis Tresham, had a brother, Lord Monteagle, in the House of Lords. Tresham sent a secret letter warning his brother that a "terrible blow" was to be delivered against Parliament and adding "yet they shall not see who hurts them".

Monteagle took the letter to the King's ministers. On November 4th they had the cellars at Westminster searched and Guy Fawkes was discovered there with his gunpowder.

Gunpowder Plot?

DUCKING STOOLS

Ducking stools first came into use as a punishment for women at the beginning of the 17th Century and were used in England as late as the beginning of the 19th. A ducking stool was a wooden armchair fastened to the end of a long wooden beam fixed like a seesaw on the edge of a river or pond. Sometimes it was mounted on wheels so that it could be pushed through the streets.

The stool was used to punish nagging wives, witches and prostitutes. An iron band kept the victim from falling out of the chair when it was plunged under the water. It was the duty of magistrates to order the number of duckings a woman should be given.

Another type of ducking stool was a chair on two wheels with two long shafts fixed to the axles. When the stool was pushed into the pond and the shafts were released the seat was tipped up backwards, but, in this case, the woman was not fastened in.

INCAS

The Incas, a race of South American Indians, are believed to have started their rise to power in Peru about five hundred years before the arrival of the Spanish conquerors in the 16th Century. They are said to have climbed into the Andes mountains from the eastern forests calling themselves "children of the Sun".

According to their favourite legend, Manco Capac, the founder of the race, came out of Lake Titicaca in Peru with his sister who was also his wife. The sun god was said to have given him a staff and told him to build a city at a spot where it sank into the ground—in other words, where the ground was fertile. This city was given the name Cuzco, meaning navel, because the Incas regarded it as the centre of the earth.

It was not long before the Incas began to conquer or absorb the neighbouring tribes. By 1460 their empire extended from the Amazon forests to the Pacific Ocean, from the borders of what is now Ecuador, deep into Chile. This 2,000-mile territory was governed by a mild form of despotism. The term Inca properly applied only to the upper caste of the nobility and those of royal blood.

Property was held in common, money was not used and the products of labour were divided in three equal portions between the church, the governing classes and the people. Inca skills included the spinning of woollen clothes, mining, engineering with tin and copper tools, the fashioning of gold and silver ornaments, irrigation and the use of fertilizers.

They used a system of writing by means of knots tied in lengths of string.

The doom of this thriving and industrious civilization was sealed when the Spanish adventurer Francisco Pizarro sailed from the Isthmus of Panama with fewer than 200 men in 1531 to conquer and loot the country. Pizarro seized the Inca ruler Atahualpa and had him put to death after accepting a vast gold and silver ransom for his life. With their leader executed and their chiefs slain, the people were forced into submission. Slaughter, plunder and oppression followed. But today the remains of massive stone temples and palaces survive as reminders of the high state of Inca culture. Like the mask above, ornaments have also survived.

WHEN were submarines first used?

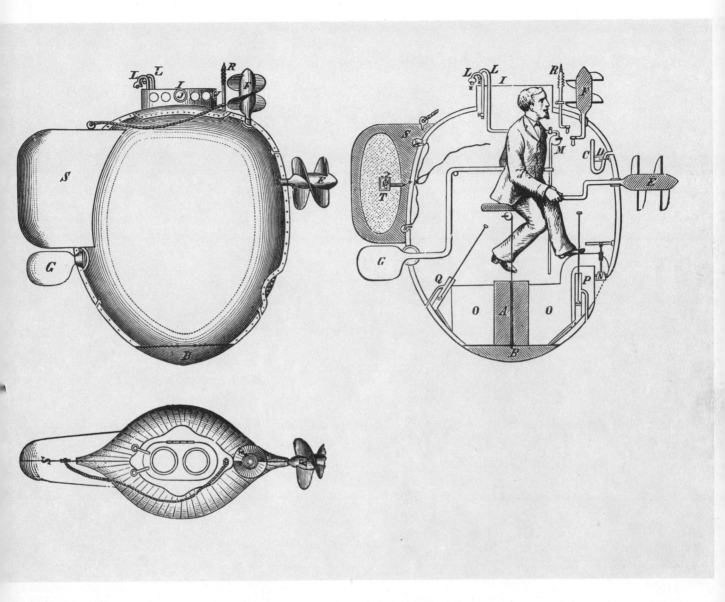

David Bushnell's remarkable submarine "Turtle". I Entry hatch O Water ballast N Water inlet P,Q Water outlets and pumps E Screw propeller for forward movement F Screw propeller for vertical movement G Rudder C,D Indicator for angle of dive L Breathing snorkel M Ventilator S Mine T Trigger charge R Screw for fixing mine to ship's bottom A,B Ballast

SUBMARINES

The first submarine which we know to have been used was built by a Dutchman, Cornelius van Drebel, in 1620. It was constructed of greased leather stretched over a wooden frame and was propelled by oars extended through the sides and sealed with tight-fitting leather flaps. Hand vices were employed to contract the sides of the vessel and reduce its volume, thus causing it to submerge. King James I of England is said to have gone for a ride in it, 12 to 15 feet below the surface of the River Thames.

But the first use of a submarine as a weapon occurred during the American War of Independence. In 1776 the Turtle, a one-man wooden submarine with a screw propeller, invented by an American, David Bushnell, tried unsuccessfully to sink a British man-of-war in New York harbour.

Attempts to build an under-water craft were made as far back as the days of ancient Greece. But practical designs had to wait for the invention of the internal combustion engine and the electric motor at the end of the 19th Century. The first truly successful submarine to travel under the sea in rough weather was the Argonaught, a 36-foot, cigar-shaped vessel built by an American, Simon Lake, in 1897. It was driven by a 30 horse-power engine.

COLOSSEUM

The great Flavian Amphitheatre, or Colosseum, was built between A.D. 69 and 81 by the Emperors Vespasian and Titus on the site of an artificial lake in the grounds of Nero's palace, the Golden House. The name Colosseum was bestowed on it, because of its colossal size, some time after the 8th Century.

In its full magnificence the Colosseum must have been one of the most imposing buildings in the Roman Empire, a gigantic oval measuring 620 feet by 513 feet with a height of 160 feet. Round the actual arena—287 feet by 180 feet—tiers of marble seats pro-vided accommodation for 50,000 spectators.

The building was constructed to house gigantic spectacles organized by the authorities for the entertainment—and distraction—of the public. It became a scene of much bloodshed. Here were staged gladiatorial combats

epression?

DEPRESSION

The American Depression began in September 1929 with a great collapse of the stock market in Wall Street, New York. During the money-making mania which accompanied the great prosperity of the 1920s, "paper" fortunes were made and the prices of shares soared to record high levels.

President Herbert Hoover tried unsuccessfully to abate the fever. On September 7 a reaction set in and on October 24 came the great Wall Street crash. On that Black Thursday, 13,000 million shares of stock were sold and prices plunged faster than ever before.

Huge fortunes were lost by many businessmen, and the savings of millions of small investors vanished. Factories were closed, the number of unemployed rocketed, foreign trade fell, banks failed, mortgages were foreclosed and, all the time, the prices of wheat, cotton, copper, oil and other commodities kept sinking. The buying power of the United States was paralysed.

These were the days of "Buddy, can you spare a dime?". All over the country people lined up at emergency "soup kitchens". Young men rode freight trains looking for work and old people died of starvation. By February 1932 a full third of the American workforce was idle. The rest of the world, too, was affected and international trade dwindled to a third of its 1928 volume.

In 1933 a new president, Franklin D. Roosevelt (1933–1945) was elected. He launched the New Deal and set up a vast system of public works paid for by the state. Contractors' orders for these schemes revived heavy industry, and workers' wages restored prosperity to the towns. Trade unions were encouraged, tariffs lowered and many laws passed which helped to save the economy.

(fights to the death between men) and contests between wild beasts or between men and animals. And here, too, many of the early Christians met martyrdom with a courage that helped greatly to spread their faith.

The highest tiers of seats and the fourth storey were rebuilt in the 3rd Century, and the building was seriously damaged by lightning and earthquakes during Roman times and the Middle Ages. For hundreds of years this symbol of Roman power was used as a quarry. But even today its ruins form one of the most famous buildings in the world.

34

WHEN were America and England last at war? WHEN we

AT WAR

American and England were last at war with each other from June 1812 to December 1814. War broke out for two reasons: first, America's expanding trade was threatened because the British were maintaining a blockade to prevent supplies reaching the French, with whom they were at war; secondly, there was a growing sense of nationalism in America, a feeling that she must fight to preserve her independence, sovereignty and honour.

When war was declared by President Madison, the Americans immediately invaded Canada, but were driven back. In 1813, after talk of an armistice came to nothing, more skirmishes broke out on the Canadian border and British sailors began to raid the American coast. By October 1814 it became clear that the Americans could not successfully invade Canada, while the British Navy could do no more than harry the coasts of America.

The chief sufferers were the merchants of New England. Also the financial state of the American government was so bad that it had no money to pay its bills abroad. Governor Strong of Massachusetts openly spoke against the war, and was suspected of planning to take his state over to the British.

However, no one in Britain wanted to fight the War of Independence all over again. The desire was to trade with and not to fight against the United States. On December 24, 1814 the Treaty of Ghent was signed and the war was over. Neither side gained.

HUMAN SACRIFICES

Human sacrifices have been made throughout history. But seldom have they been so terrible as the ceremonies associated with the barbarous religion of the Aztecs who began to establish their civilization in present-day Mexico in about 1168.

The Aztecs, who in many other respects were a comparatively enlightened people, believed that human bloodshed was the way to make sure that the sun would rise each day. At one of their biggest sacrificial ceremonies about 20,000 people were slaughtered.

The chief places for sacrifice were two great pyramid temples, 100 feet high, in the capital city of Tenochtitlan, which was built on an island in the middle of a lake.

An Aztec warrior's chief aim in battle was to take his enemy prisoner and hand him over for sacrifice to his war-god. On the day chosen for the ceremony the war drums were sounded and the prisoners were taken, one by one, up the winding stairs round the outside of the temple to the altar. Here their chests were cut open and their hearts torn out as offerings to the sun. Afterwards some of their bodies were eaten at ritual feasts.

The great empire of the Aztecs, stretching from the deserts of northern Mexico to the tropical forests of Guatemala, seemed to be at the height of its splendour when the Spanish conqueror Hernando Cortez landed with a tiny army from Cuba in March, 1519. After being treated as gods, the invaders were attacked and nearly destroyed. But within two years the Aztec ruler Montezuma was slain by his people and his empire overthrown by Cortez.

uman sacrifices made? **WHEN** was slavery abolished?

WHEN was the auto-da-fé?

SLAVERY

The first big step to rid the world of slavery was taken in 1811 when Britain abolished slave-trading. In 1833 an Act of Parliament was passed emancipating all slaves in the British colonies, thus setting an example which was followed by other European countries.

In the United States a number of conflicting interests led in 1861 to a civil war between the Northern states who wished to abolish slavery and the seceded Southern states who wanted to retain it on the plantations. In 1863 President Lincoln issued his famous Emancipation Proclamation, and two years later the victory of the North led to a constitutional amendment which prohibited slavery in the United States for ever.

In South America, a kind of agricultural slavery of the Indians continued under the name of peonage, and laws prohibiting the system did not succeed immediately in stamping it out. Even today conditions of slavery, sometimes disguised as forced labour in payment of debt, exist in some countries.

Until people's consciences began to be stirred by the efforts of humanitarians like William Wilberforce (1759–1833), slavery had generally been regarded as an inevitable part of the natural order of things. From earliest times men had forced their captured enemies to work for them. Slaves were a vital part of most ancient civilizations, providing food and services for their masters and the labour to build such man-made marvels as the pyramids. In Greece and Rome many slaves became skilled workers and held responsible positions.

After the discovery of the New World large fortunes were made by the transport of Negroes from Africa and their exploitation in the Americas.

AUTO-DA-FÉ

The auto-da-fé (act of faith) was the name of the public ceremony which followed the secret trials of the Spanish Inquisition established in 1478 during the reign of King Ferdinand of Aragon and Queen Isabella of Castile.

These two Christian monarchs, having united most of Spain by their marriage, were about to complete the age-old battle to free the country from "the infidels" by the conquest of Granada from the Moors. The time was ripe for them to seek to encourage national unity and strengthen the authority both of themselves and of the Church.

So it was a mixture of motives that led Ferdinand and Isabella to persuade Pope Sixtus IV to set up the Spanish Inquisition, with the declared purpose of disciplining the flourishing and influential Jewish community, whose wealth aroused envy and whose presence seemed to offer the greatest obstacle to unity. Soon the powers of the Inquisition (from the Latin *inquiro*, to inquire into) were directed not only against Jews but also against Moors, Christian Pro-

testants and even Catholics whose behaviour was deemed to threaten the solidarity of the Church on which the royal authority also rested.

After secret interrogations, sometimes aided by torture, the auto-da-fé was celebrated. First came a procession of priests, officials and accused persons who had confessed their guilt and declared themselves penitent. This was followed by a solemn mass, an oath of obedience to the Inquisition and the reading of sentences whether of punishment or acquittal. Those condemned to death were handed over to the civil power to emphasize the fact that the Church did not itself shed blood.

But the severity of the first Grand Inquisitor, Tomás de Torquemada (1420–1498) is thought to have led to 2,000 burnings at the stake and unsuccessful attempts at mediation by the Pope.

After the reigns of Ferdinand's successors, Charles I (1516–56) and Philip II (1556–98), the Inquisition gradually dwindled in influence and was finally suppressed in 1834.

36

WHEN did Ghenghis Khan live? WHEN was the Black Deat

WHEN wa

GENGHIS KHAN

Genghis Khan was born in 1155, 1162 or—more likely—1167. We cannot date his birth with certainty, but we do know that he died in 1227. He was a Mongolian, a member of a small group of clans in Outer Mongolia (now the Mongolian People's Republic) north of China.

As a boy he was named Temujin, but he grew up to be such an able soldier that he was acclaimed by his followers in 1206 as "Genghis Khan". The new name probably meant Ocean Chief, using the word ocean as meaning wide or encompassing.

A series of conquests made him undisputed leader of all the nomad, or wandering, tribes of the district. He campaigned against the Kin dynasty of Manchuria and eastern North China in 1211–1214 and reached Peking.

Leaving further conquest in China to his generals, he turned his attention to the west, where his most distant and ambitious campaign, from 1219–1225, carried him through Turkestan into Persia, Afghanistan, Azerbaijan, the Caucasus and south Russia.

Genghis Khan's ferocity became a byword, for he used living citizens as shield walls for his troops and deliberately massacred thousands of prisoners to frighten cities into surrendering. His last campaign was to the kingdom of Tanggut, called by the Chinese Hsi-Hsia, which lay across the Yellow River in Kanon Province. In the course of it the Khan died, partly from the effects of a fall while hunting.

He was particularly clever at psychological warfare and made many secret alliances, which he was careful to break only when he had made sure that he could justify his action to the satisfaction of his more important allies.

WASHINGTON D.C.

Washington D.C. (District of Columbia), named after the first American president, George Washington, was made the capital of the United States when Congress, the American parliament, met there in the middle of November, 1800.

The United States was the first nation in the world to plan a capital city especially for its seat of government. Her example has been followed in this century by Australia, Pakistan and Brazil. Before 1800 Congress sat in eight cities—Philadelphia, Baltimore, Lancaster, York, Princeton, Trenton, Annapolis and New York— and competition was keen to secure the seat of government.

In 1790 it was decided that the capital city should be a district not exceeding 10 square miles on the Potomac River "at some place between the mouths of the Eastern Branch and the Connogocheague".

On September 18, 1793, George Washington laid the cornerstone of the presidential palace. It was built of Virginia freestone (limestone), a material so white that, as early as 1809, people began to speak of it as the White House.

The present day Washington covers an area of about 69 square miles.

BLACK DEATH

The Black Death was a plague that raged through Europe from 1347–1350. It was caused by fleas living on rats which were carried to Europe from Asia by Genoese trading ships. It is suggested that the Black Death was probably bubonic plague, that is to say the sufferers developed "buboes" or inflamed swellings.

About one in three Europeans died of the disease. The sudden decrease in population brought serious social problems. An acute labour shortage led to higher wages and there was a short-lived slump in trade. Many people became obsessed with the idea of death, for there were many recurrences of the plague, notably during the years 1361–3, 1369–71, 1374–5, 1390 and 1400.

On the other hand, the plague speeded changes that had already begun, changes which had their roots in growing trade and the increasing use of money. It be- came profitable to export wool and wheat. So land gained a new importance, and many nobles, who had lost labourers and were forced to pay much higher wages to those remaining, chose to sell their estates land to rich merchants. Thus arose a new class of landowners where wealth counted as much as birth.

The population of western Europe did not regain its pre-1348 level until the beginning of the 16th Century.

3

Washington D.C. made the capital of the United States?

The White House, Washington, at sunset with the Jefferson Memorial behind.

WHEN did the Vikings reach America?
WHEN was Charlemagne crowned Holy Roman

VIKINGS

The Vikings discovered America about the year 1000, more than four centuries before Christopher Columbus was born. They were sea adventurers from Scandinavia who left their homes in search of conquest and plunder.

Information about the Viking discoveries comes from two sagas, or narrative ballads, the *Saga of Eric the Red* and the *Saga of the Greenlanders*. These differ considerably, but it seems possible that Bjarni Herjolfsson discovered North America in 986, when driven off course on a voyage from Iceland to Greenland. About 1000, Leif Ericsson sailed west from Greenland and gave the names Helluland, Markland and Vinland to sections of the American coast as he moved south. A few years later Thorfinn Karlsefni sailed for Vinland with three ships, with a party of settlers and domestic animals. But they stayed only three years.

The so-called Vinland Map, discovered and published in 1965, dates from 1431–1449 and supports the theory that Herjolfsson originally discovered America. In 1961 a Viking-style settlement was discovered at L'Anse au Meadow, Newfoundland. The Vinland Map itself is now held by some experts to be a clever fake.

CHARLEMAGNE

Charlemagne (Charles the Great) was crowned Holy Roman Emperor at St Peter's Basilica in Rome on Christmas Day in the year 800.

It is one of the most important dates in the Middle Ages, the beginning of a new era in European history. The man thus charged with the task of restoring order and unity out of the chaos which had followed the downfall of Christian Rome was already an emperor in fact, though not in name.

When his ally Pope Leo III placed the crown on Charles's head—unexpectedly, it was said, while he knelt in prayer—this heir to the Caesars already ruled lands stretching from Denmark to Rome and from the Atlantic to the Danube.

Charlemagne was born in 742, the grandson of Charles Martel who, 10 years before, had saved Christendom from the Saracens at the Battle of Tours in France. At the age of 26 he inherited the kingdom of the Franks and set out to bring order to western Europe and Christianity to heathen tribes. At the time of his death in 814 he had extended his rule from the Baltic Sea to the Pyrenees and from the coast of Brittany eastwards across Germany and Italy to the lower valley of the Danube.

Although he never learned to write, Charlemagne did much to encourage education and the arts. After his death the Frankish empire broke into pieces. About 130 years later the Holy Roman Empire was again revived and lasted with dwindling power until its extinction in 1806. But the fragmentation of western Europe persisted through the centuries with continual outbreaks of warfare up to the end of the Second World War.

The picture at the top was done by Albrecht Durer in 1510. It shows Charlemagne dressed as a German emperor.

RENAISSANCE

The name "renaissance" means rebirth. It was given to the revival of learning that began among the educated classes of northern Italy in the early 14th Century, developed and spread in 15th and 16th Centuries to the rest of Europe.

One important feature of the Renaissance set it apart from the period that had gone before. This was an amazing rebirth of interest in the thought, literature, sculpture and architecture of Greece and Rome. Two of the greatest names associated with the arts at this time are those of Leonardo da Vinci (1452–1519) and Michelangelo (1475–1564).

Men began to look about them in a more questioning way, politics assumed a new importance, and the way was opened for the great scientific discoveries of later years.

In Mainz, Germany, about the middle of the 15th Century, Johann Gutenberg invented a printing process using movable type which made possible the widespread distribution of books. It was a Christian Renaissance, summed up in the life and work of Desiderius Erasmus (1466–1536) of Holland. Among the literary giants of the later Renaissance were William Shakespeare (1564–1616) in England and Miguel de Cervantes (1547–1616) in Spain.

The Renaissance inspired the curiosity of hundreds of explorers who took part in the Great Age of Discovery. Christopher Columbus, Vasco da Gama, Ferdinand Magellan and others voyaged across the seas to discover the New World and to open up the longed-for trading routes to Asia. Trade prospered and powerful banking houses stimulated the growth of capitalism.

Detail from a drawing by Michelangelo, one of the greatest artists and sculptors of the Renaissance.

mperor? **WHEN** was the Renaissance?

This richly coloured painting of the Nativity is by Domenico Ghirlandaio.

BIRTH OF JESUS

Although the Christian calendar is nominally dated from the year of Christ's birth, modern researchers have placed the actual year between 4 and 7 B.C. When the calendar was changed the monk Dionysius Exiguus (500–600) set the date of "the incarnation of the Lord" as the year 753 after the founding of the city of Rome. But his arithmetic was inaccurate.

The Gospels say that Jesus was born while Herod was on the throne, and Herod died about 749, according to the Roman calendar, or about 4 B.C. Also the census mentioned by St Luke as the reason why Joseph and Mary travelled to Bethlehem seems to have been held in the Roman year 747, or 6 B.C.

HAMLET

Hamlet, the hero of Shakespeare's great tragedy, seems to correspond to a figure called Amleth, who appears in a history of Denmark, written by Saxo Grammaticus late in the 12th Century.

However, it is impossible to say whether he did in fact exist. The figure of the young man whose father was murdered by a brother who later married his victim's widow appears in many legends. In all of them the son pretends to be mad in order to revenge his father's death. Such stories are found as far back as the Icelandic saga of Amlöoi, mentioned by the 10th Century poet, Snaebjörn.

The story of Hamlet is told in the fifth volume of *Histoires Tragiques* (1570) by François de Belleforest and an English version of this, *The Hystorie of Hamblet* was published in London in 1608. Shakespeare's tragedy was written about 1601, but a play about Hamlet believed to have been written by Thomas Kyd was performed in about 1509.

Kronborg Castle—Hamlet's Elsinore.

As he often did, Shakespeare borrowed the plot from others and transformed it by his genius into a great work of art.

CRUSADES

The Crusades were a series of holy wars authorized by successive Popes and waged by the Christians of western Europe from 1095 to the end of the 13th Century. Their purpose was the recovery of the Holy Sepulchre in Jerusalem and other sacred places from the Mohammedans. The word comes from the Spanish *cruzada*, meaning "marked with a cross".

There were three basic causes for the Crusades: first, the threat to pilgrims journeying to the Holy Sepulchre from the Seljuk Turks who had overrun Anatolia, Syria and Palestine; secondly, a great surge of energy in Christianized western Europe and a desire to expand territory and control trade routes; thirdly, the determination of the Church to make its authority universal.

The First Crusade, summoned by Pope Urban II in 1095, took Jerusalem by storm on July 15, 1099 and set up Christian governments in the city and in the three "Latin states" of Edessa, Antioch and Tripoli. When Edessa was captured by the Mohammedans in 1144, Pope Eugenius III called the Second Crusade (1147–1149), but this was so mismanaged that it accomplished nothing.

The recapture of Jerusalem in 1187 by the wise, brave and chivalrous Mohammedan leader Saladin gave rise to the Third Crusade (1189–1191) led by Philip the Fair of France and Richard the Lion-Hearted of England. In the Holy Land Acre was captured but the two kings quarrelled and first Philip and then Richard abandoned the struggle. The Fourth Crusade (1202–1204) never reached Palestine but instead attacked and captured the Christian city of Constantinople. The Fifth Crusade (1221) was a complete failure but on the Sixth Crusade (1228–1229) Jerusalem was obtained from the Mohammedans by negotiation. The city's capture by the Turks in 1244 brought the Seventh Crusade (1249) in which the leader King Louis IX of France was taken prisoner and ransomed. Louis also led the Eighth Crusade, this time to Tunis where he died of the plague in 1270. The knights held out in Acre until 1291 when they surrendered. Attempts to revive the Holy Wars in the 14th Century failed.

WHEN was gas first used in war?　WHEN does Moder
WHEN was keelhauling used as a method of punishment

German soldiers advance in gas masks.

GAS IN WAR

Gas was, perhaps, first used in battle in the Peloponnesian War between Sparta and Athens (431–404 B.C.) when burning pitch and sulphur were used to produce suffocating gases. But poison gas as a modern weapon was introduced in the First World War on April 22, 1915. The Germans then launched a cylinder attack with chlorine against the British and French at Ypres.

Later many varieties of war gas were introduced. In July 1917 the Germans began using mustard gas, which caused severe, slow-healing burns on the skin and damage to the lungs. Many casualties resulted from gas bombardment, but relatively few people died. Both sides were ready to use increased gas attacks when the war ended in 1918.

During the Second World War and the Korean War gas was not used, but preparations were carried out by both sides. Perhaps the most terrifying discovery was made by the Germans. This was a new series of chemical agents called nerve gases which rapidly result in convulsions, coma and—unless promptly treated—death.

Tear gas, which causes intense smarting and watering of the eyes is used in many countries to control rioting crowds, but its effects are only temporary.

KEELHAULING

Keelhauling was first referred to as a punishment for offenders in a Dutch naval ordinance of 1560. It was carried out in the British Navy at least as early as the first half of the 17th Century.

The punishment consisted of lowering the victim down one side of the ship and dragging him under the keel to the other side.

It was never 'official' in the British Navy but the Dutch retained it until 1853.

MODERN HISTORY

Most historians date the beginning of modern history from about the year 1500. "Modern" comes from a Latin adverb meaning "just now", and the word was applied to history as early as Elizabethan days. It meant an awareness of newness, of living in times different from those of one's ancestors.

The Renaissance, with its great revival in art and learning, the great geographical discoveries, the invention of printing, and the Reformation, with the rise of Protestantism, combined to make the start of the 16th Century a convenient time from which to date modern history.

However, it is a convenient, rather than an accurate, date.

Modern times should not be seen as a sunrise ending the medieval night. The last few centuries of the Middle Ages saw much scientific advancement, growth of trade and the establishment of a money economy. Also, many medieval ways persisted in western Europe as late as the 17th Century, including the legal system in England and the land-holding system in France.

Even today, pockets of culture can be found in out-of-the-way places which are mediaeval or pre-medieval in structure. The Middle Ages grows into the Modern Age and the 15th, 16th and 17th Centuries are perhaps best seen as centuries of transition.

istory begin?

WHEN was the Battle of Britain?

BATTLE OF BRITAIN

The Battle of Britain in the Second World War began with skirmishes in June and July 1940, reached a climax in August and September and ended in the ferocity of the Blitz during the following winter. It laid the foundations for the survival of Britain and the eventual destruction of Nazi Germany.

Soon after the fall of France in the middle of June, the Germans began to prepare for a possible invasion of Britain by setting out first to destroy the Royal Air Force. There was a long series of air battles and bombardments.

The Germans seemed to have no systematic plan of action. On the other hand, Britain had developed a radar early warning system and a superb fighting aircraft, the Spitfire. Thus, although outnumbered, the British were able to defend with superior equipment and undivided aim against an enemy whose fleets of bombers, the Dornier 17, the Heinkel III and the Junkers 88, proved vulnerable to attacks by Spitfires and Hurricanes. The best German fighter, the Messerschmitt 109, was on a par with the Spitfire but, over England, was at the limit of its range.

After waves of attacks had failed to put the R.A.F. out of action, the Germans switched their offensive from Fighter Command airfields and installations to London and other cities, causing terrible damage. But the raiders also suffered heavy casualties. On September 15 the British destroyed 185 enemy aircraft, demonstrating to the Luftwaffe, the German air force, that it had lost the battle. Attacks on cities with explosive and fire bombs continued but lost their impetus by the end of April 1941.

Bombs dropping near St. Paul's Cathedral, London, in 1940.

JEWISH DIASPORA

Diaspora is the name given to Jewish communities who over thousands of years established themselves in different parts of the world. It is a Greek word meaning scattering.

The history of diaspora goes back to the 8th Century B.C. when the people of Judah in northern Palestine were taken to captivity in Babylon on the River Euphrates in modern Iraq. When the exile ended after about 200 years a great number of their descendants remained behind and formed a community, or diaspora, which continued to be important until the middle of the 11th Century.

The next great diaspora period occurred after the death of Alexander the Great in 323 B.C. when attempts by his successors to impose Greek authority on Jewish customs in Palestine led to thousands of Jews choosing exile. This period saw the formation of the great diaspora in Alexandria, Egypt. Here in the first century B.C. more than 40 per cent of the population were Jews who had learned to combine Greek ideas with their own to produce a flourishing culture.

But the biggest dispersal from Palestine took place under the Roman Empire, especially after A.D. 70 when the army of Titus, later Roman emperor, crushed a nationalist revolt and destroyed the temple in Jerusalem. Although financial help from exiled patriots continued, Palestine gradually ceased to be a Jewish state. In the following centuries the "scattering" spread throughout the world.

In 1939 the estimated number of Jews in the world was 16 million, of whom about 475,000 were in Palestine. Horror and pity aroused by the systematic destruction of Jews by Nazi Germany led indirectly to the creation of the state of Israel in 1948.

CONVICTS

The last convicts were sent to Australia in 1849. They arrived in a ship called the Hashemy, the first convicts to arrive in the colony since 1840. The Hashemy docked in Melbourne, but public protests against the landing of the prisoners caused the authorities to move the ship on to Sydney. There the public outcry was even greater and the Hashemy sailed to Brisbane, where the convicts were put ashore.

The protests arose because many Australians, especially tradespeople and wage earners, were bitterly opposed to the continued flow of free labour to the colony. But transportation (the sending of convicts) was still favoured by sheep owners and farmers, who wanted the labour, and by the British Government, who found it a cheap way of getting rid of unwanted citizens.

After the convicts from the Hashemy had finally disembarked, anti-transportation leagues were formed and attracted so much public support that it was decided to send no more convicts to any part of the colony.

An early engraving of a convict chain gang in Australia.

MIDDLE AGES

The Middle Ages in Europe can be regarded as lasting roughly from about 800 to 1500, or from the times of Charlemagne to those of Columbus. The changes that came about in that period were largely due to the growth of towns and the increase in trade. The Mediterranean area, especially, was opened up by new routes over land, river and sea. Bartering, o the exchange of one kind of goods for another, gave way to the use o money.

Outside the towns, the socia classes in Europe were mainly o three kinds: the church, the nobility or warrior class, and the peasants who worked the land Feudalism was the pattern o

A monk at work—from a medieval illuminated manuscript.

society. The word comes from the Latin *feudum*, meaning a piece of land granted in return for services.

The nobles held the land and it was leased to freemen or worked by serfs (labourers "bound to the soil" who could not leave their master's estate). The feudal system began to weaken about the end of the 13th Century, and meanwhile the trading classes were growing in wealth and power.

The Roman Catholic Church became an international power, as missionaries followed in the footsteps of the traders, but its authority did not go unchallenged. By fighting the Church and one another, medieval kings awoke national feelings in their peoples and laid the foundation for the separate nation-states of Europe.

Nevertheless, during the Middle Ages, Europe—especially western Europe—felt a sense of unity which it did not again experience until the present time. This was due to a common religion and to a common use of Latin.

WHEN was Pearl Harbor? WHEN was Persepolis destroye WHEN does war escalate?

PEARL HARBOR

The Japanese bombing raids on Pearl Harbor, Hawaii, which led to the entry of the United States into the Second World War, were made about breakfast time on December 7, 1941. In a little over an hour and without even a declaration of war, Japan crippled the American Pacific fleet and made possible the conquest or domination of large areas of land and sea.

Relations between the United States and Japan had been strained for at least 10 years. Although neither country had yet taken an active part in the great conflict, their sympathies were on opposite sides. Japan had signed an agreement with Germany and Italy, while the United States was supplying Britain.

America's Pacific fleet of nearly 100 vessels, including eight battleships, had been stationed at Pearl Harbor since April 1940, and the commanders there had been warned of the possibility of war. However, when the attack came, it took the Americans almost completely by surprise.

At 7.55 am local time their warships and protective airfields were attacked by 200 Japanese aircraft, including torpedo planes, bombers

and fighters. At 8.50 am a second attack began and lasted just over 10 minutes.

When it was all over the Americans counted their losses; more than 2,000 sailors and 200 Army personnel killed; three battleships destroyed, a fourth capsized, a fifth

heavily damaged and the remaining three lightly damaged; two light cruisers and three destroyers among other ships also damaged, 42 aircraft destroyed and 41 damaged.

The Japanese had lost 29 aircraft and five midget submarines.

PERSEPOLIS

Persepolis, the ancient capital of Darius the Great, king of the Persians, was partly destroyed by Alexander the Great, the celebrated king of Macedonia who overthrew the Persian empire and conquered large sections of India.

The great palace of Darius was by all accounts a marvellous building and the surviving ruins are a tribute to its vast size. Situated some thirty miles northeast of Shirez in southwest Iran, the ruins consist of retaining walls up to more than forty feet in height and a truly splendid double stair of 111 stone steps ascending to a terrace.

There are the remains of a number of once enormous buildings on this terrace. The buildings are built from huge slabs of highly polished grey stone beautifully cut and laid together without the aid of mortar. The remains of Darius's great audience hall can still be seen, with its huge stone columns. Thirteen of these are still standing.

Alexander had long vowed to destroy the might of Darius and the burning of Persepolis was a symbol of Greek revenge against the Persians. Some sources say that the burning of the great palace was encouraged by a courtesan

at a drunken celebration. But undoubtedly it was symbolic of the triumph of the Greeks.

Alexander was one of the greatest generals in history. He was a pupil of Aristotle, the great Greek philosopher, and was keenly interested in scientific exploration. Indeed, his invasion of India was largely inspired by his desire to explore. His achievements—and he was only 32 when he died—were truly enormous. He spread the influence of Greek thought and civilization from Gibraltar to India and he created the city of Alexandria in Egypt.

4

WHEN did West Point start?
WHEN was the Battle of Agincourt?

WEST POINT

West Point, the United States military academy for the training of regular army officers was established on March 16, 1802 at West Point on the Hudson River about 50 miles north of the city of New York. The place was already famous as the scene, 22 years earlier, of a dramatic incident in the War of Independence, when the traitor Benedict Arnold failed in an attempt to betray the strategically important position to the British.

Three chief reasons for the formation of the academy were: first, the fact that in the War of Independence the United States had been forced to rely on foreign military technicians; second, the belief of army leaders, including George Washington, that military techniques must be studied and not acquired solely through experience; third, the desire of some reformers for a new approach to the education of officers.

In 1812 the academy, which had been training only engineers, was reorganized and given more scope. In 1866 an Act of Congress was passed to allow the selection of an academy superintendent who was not an engineer.

West Point is under the direct control of the army and the four-year course of instruction leads to a science degree and a commission of second lieutenant in the regular army. Studies are balanced between mathematics and engineering sciences (55 per cent) and the humanities and social sciences (45 per cent). The 3,100 cadets must be between 17 and 22 years old and unmarried, with a high school education. Aptitude tests and a medical examination must be passed before admission.

ESCALATION

War is said to escalate when it increases rapidly in scale or intensity. The word was added to the military vocabulary by the Americans during the Vietnam War to denote the increasing degrees of United States involvement in the fighting. It has also been used by military writers to describe the development of a possible war between two powers through successive stages from the use of conventional weapons to the localized employment of atomic weapons and, finally, an all-out exchange of annihilating nuclear missiles.

It is a far cry from the use of the word escalator by the American Jesse W. Reno to describe the moving staircase he invented in 1891. Both words come from the Spanish *escalada*, meaning the scaling of the walls of a fortress by means of ladders. A staircase moving inevitably upwards provides a more fitting image than a scaling ladder of the horrifying expansion of which war today is capable.

BATTLE OF AGINCOURT

The Battle of Agincourt took place on October 25, 1415, near the village of Agincourt in the Pas-de-Calais, France. The battle was one of the most notable in history and is particularly famous for the havoc wrought on the French by the longbowmen of England.

The English army was led by King Henry V. He had already taken Harfleur in Normandy and his plan was to return to England via Calais. However, this plan was thwarted when he discovered that his road to the port was blocked by the French army.

Henry's men had marched and fought for many days. They were tired and short of food. The king knew he must give battle.

Although the English were outnumbered by three to one, the French had sandwiched themselves in between two areas of woodland which made it difficult for them to deploy their troops in the narrow space of open land. Henry cleverly stationed his force of some 5,000 archers towards one end of the woods and other archers protected groups of men-at-arms.

The French were greatly hampered on the soggy land by their heavy armour. After a devastating archery assault—the air was said to be dark with English arrows—the archers were ordered to move in for the kill and to attack with axe and sword. The French lost about 10,000 men and were completely routed. English casualties were light—about 1,500 men. It was at Agincourt that the power of the longbow reached its supreme point.

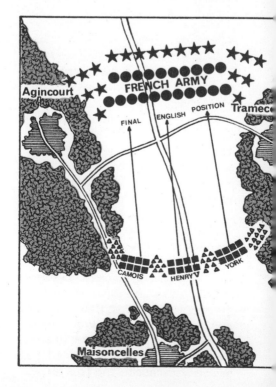

This old Greek amphora shows a story from the Iliad—Odysseus piercing the single eye of the giant Polyphemus.

ILIAD

According to ancient Greek tradition the Iliad was written by the poet Homer (8th–7th Century B.C.). He was said to have been the author of many epic or heroic poems, of which only the Iliad, the story of the siege of Troy, and the Odyssey, the story of Odysseus' wanderings, survive.

The "Homeric question", the attempt which has gone on ever since to find out whether Homer really existed, and, if he did, whether he wrote the poetry, began towards the end of the 6th Century B.C. The first to inquire into the matter was Theagenes of Rhegium. Two writers in the early 7th Century B.C. mention Homer as a poet, but the first person to name his poems was the historian Herodotus in the 5th Century B.C.

What little information is available about Homer suggests that he was born in Smyrna about 740 B.C., trained as a bard (a singer-poet) and travelled about the Greek world until he went blind. Then he settled on the island of Chios and gathered pupils about him. He is believed to have composed the Iliad and perhaps the Odyssey towards the end of his life and to have died about 670 B.C. while on a visit to the island of Ios.

The works credited to him were admired so much by later Greeks that they often referred to him simply as "the poet". The Iliad and the Odyssey are among the greatest works of world literature.

ook written?   WHEN was the French Revolution?

HISTORY BOOK

Herodotus, a Greek author, known as the "father of history" was born some time in the 5th Century B.C. His book *History*, describing the wars between Greece and Persia, is generally considered to be the first deliberate attempt to see the events of the time against a historical background.

"I am giving," he says in his opening words, "the results of my inquiries (*historai*) so that the memory of what men have done shall not perish from the world nor their achievements, whether of Greeks or of foreigners, go unsung. They form my theme, and the cause why they went to war."

The *History* is told as a story, using conversation, tragedy and humour. Herodotus was a great traveller with an eye for detail and, on the whole, a good geographer. He was intensely interested in his fellow men and his lack of prejudices makes his book not only very readable but also enormously important historically. Herodotus was also the first European writer of straightforward prose.

FRENCH REVOLUTION

The French Revolution began on July 14, 1789 with the storming of the Bastille prison in Paris, popularly regarded as a symbol of oppression and injustice. Evidence that a revolution was at hand had been provided two months earlier when King Louis XVI, a well-meaning but irresolute man, tried to solve his desperate financial problems by calling a meeting of the Estates-General, the French parliament.

When this almost forgotten body met on May 5 for the first time in 175 years, the third estate, who represented the people, defied the nobles and clergy and declared themselves the National Assembly. On June 20 they took an oath not to disperse until they had given France a constitution which would defend the middle class and peasants against the feudal aristocracy.

Spurred on by the example of the United States, people everywhere were in revolt against absolute and obsolete authority. Two years after the fall of the Bastille, the National Assembly issued the Declaration of the Rights of Man, proclaiming liberty, equality and brotherhood. Then came the flight and recapture of the royal family, and the declaration of a republic in September, 1792.

Four months later Louis was beheaded by the newly invented guillotine. For 18 months France was ruled by an extreme group,

The storming of the Bastille, July 14, 1789.

the Jacobins, who instituted the "Reign of Terror" during which thousands of people were executed, including Queen Marie Antoinette, aristocrats, deposed revolutionaries, such as Danton and Hébert, and finally, on July 28, 1794, the terror leader Robespierre himself became a victim.

France turned with relief to the moderate rule of a committee known as the Directory of Five. At length on November 9, 1799, Napoleon Bonaparte seized power. The revolution was over, leaving Europe and the world a lasting legacy of violence in the cause of liberty and equality.

Medicine and the Body

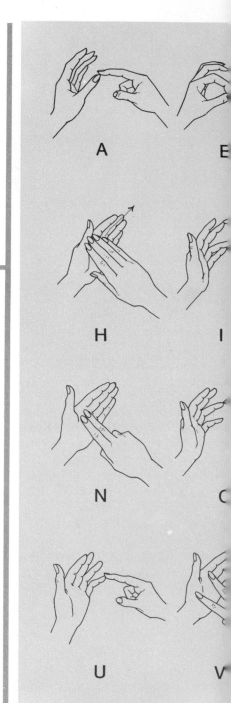

A   E

H   I

N   O

U   V

MENOPAUSE

The menopause, climacteric or "change of life" may begin for women at any time from the late 30s to early 50s, but usually occurs at around the age of 45. The menopause is the sign that the reproductive period of a woman's life is coming to a close. The female ovaries no longer produce eggs or hormones and, therefore, menstruation ceases.

From the time a woman begins to have a regular menstrual or monthly period, a single egg ripens in the ovary each month. This egg is shed from the ovary and passes down the oviduct to the womb or uterus. If the egg is not fertilized, it dies and the lining of the womb, together with some blood, is shed and passed out through the vagina. Afterwards a new lining grows, ready for the next egg.

Some women feel depressed and unwell at the time of the menopause as their bodies adjust themselves for the next phase of life. But these symptoms usually disappear with time. The length of the menopause varies.

Men also pass through a menopause when there is a marked decline in the production of sperms. But the outward symptoms are not usually very marked, and the change usually takes place later in life, between 55 and 60.

HARE LIP

A hare-lip occurs when one or both sides of the upper lip fails to fuse or join with the middle part below the nose.

In the human embryo, the nose, upper lip and palate are formed by the fusion of three separate blocks of tissue. Growing downwards from the head is the fronto-nasal process. This is the medical name given to the development of the block containing the middle of the upper lip, the nose and forehead, and the front of the hard palate. The other two blocks, which grow inwards from left and right make up the cheeks, the two sides of the upper lip and the rest of the palate. These are called the maxillary processes.

A hare-lip is usually repaired by plastic surgery for the sake of appearance. But it does not often affect a baby's ability to take nourishment and the operation is not generally carried out until the child is about three years old.

Often, however, a hare-lip is combined with a cleft palate, which occurs when the two processes that grow in towards each other to form the roof of the mouth fail to join.

This usually means an earlier operation, as otherwise the child will have great difficulty in eating and in learning to speak.

SIGN LANGUAGE

Sign language for people who could not hear or speak was developed in the 18th Century. The Abbé Charles Michel Epée (1712–1789) studied the sign language which had grown up among such people over the centuries and organized it into a systematic language which could be used in education and com-

WHEN was the sign language for deaf-mutes invented?

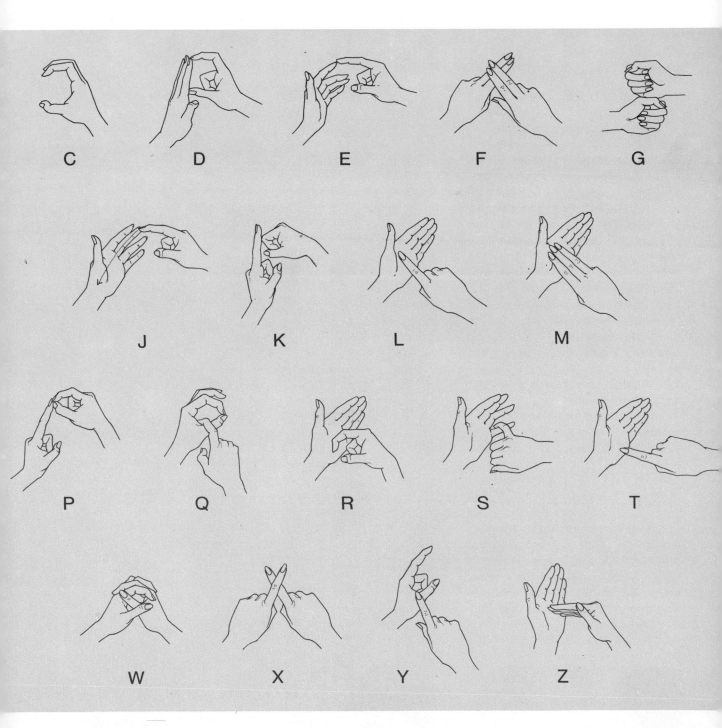

munication. His work was developed by the Abbé Sicard (1742–1822). A code of manual gestures evolved, some representing letters of the alphabet and others symbolizing whole words or phrases.

The Abbé Epée concentrated on gestures in his school for deaf-mutes, but other teachers believed that the deaf should be taught to lip-read and, if possible, to communicate by sounds. One of the greatest teachers of the latter method was the German Moritz Hill (1805–1874). Today many educators use a combination of both methods. The example of Helen Keller (1880–1968), a blind deaf-mute, who was taught to speak by a devoted teacher, Anne Sullivan, made millions of people realize that deaf-mutes failed to develop speech only because they are unable to hear other people speaking.

In the 20th Century tremendous advances have been made in the early recognition of impaired hearing and in the training of teachers and other specialists.

ACUPUNCTURE

Acupuncture originated in China as a form of medical treatment about 2,500 years ago. It has been practised by the Chinese ever since.

The treatment involves the insertion of small metal needles into one or many of 365 spots on the human body. Each of these spots, designated by ancient Chinese doctors, represents a particular function or organ of the human body. Accordingly a heart or liver line can be traced by linking the appropriate spots which relate to the particular organ. If a patient has eye trouble the needles will be inserted into his eye line, which may not necessarily come anywhere near the eye. The needles do not go deep, and are not painful. A single treatment may last only 10 minutes.

It is not clear why acupuncture works, but some scientists have suggested that the needles may relieve the nerves affecting a disease.

Since the beginning of this century the treatment has been introduced in the West. At first there was much scepticism, but recently acupuncture has been widely accepted and has been found to be not only a cure but also a valuable form of anaesthetic.

Acupuncture experts in China and Japan devised guide drawings for the positions of the punctures to cure certain complaints. These early drawings are typical of these guidelines which form a handbook for young students of the science. In acupuncture there are three main ways of pricking the needles into the skin and the material from which the needles are made is also an important point.
Altogether, classical acupuncture techniques recognize some 787 separate puncture points and all these points are carefully arranged to produce specific effects and cures.

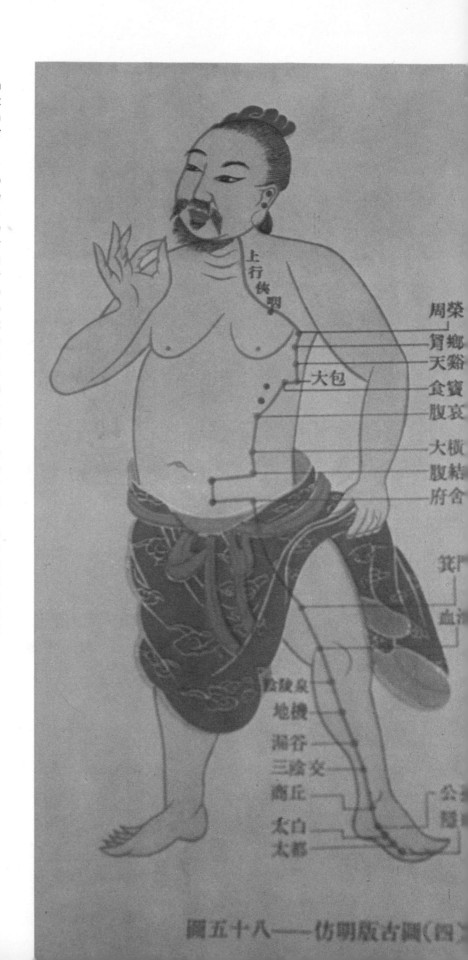

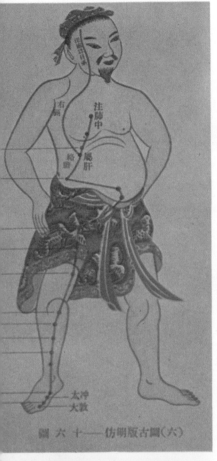

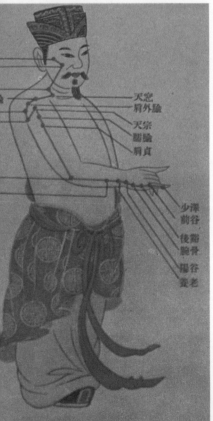

圖六十一——仿明版古圖(六)

Here are some examples of sounds and their relative intensities in decibels
0 Almost complete silence

10 Leaves rustling in a slight breeze

20 A person whispering from a few feet away

30 A quiet office room

40 Subdued conversation

50 Ordinary conversation in an office area

60 Noise in a department store

70 Continuous traffic in a street

80 Noise of subway trains

90 Pneumatic drill close by

100 Metal drill

110 Hi-fi equipment at 10 watts

120 Aeroplane propeller at 16,000 r.p.m.

SOUNDS THAT HURT

Sounds hurt the ears when they register about 130 on the decibel scale. Decibels are units for measuring the loudness of sound. They show how strong the sound waves are.

The lightest sound—perhaps that of a butterfly landing—would register about zero on the decibel scale; the noise level of a house with the television turned on would be about 50; the din in a car factory would measure 95 or more; and some amplified pop music may be near the limit where the ears would be hurt.

Sound waves are formed by millions of molecules of air bumping and vibrating against one another. Weak sound waves move the eardrum only slightly, but strong ones cause it to respond violently and, in time, may damage hearing permanently. The waves get weaker the further they travel.

The word decibel was coined by scientists in honour of Alexander Graham Bell whose interest in sound waves led to the invention of the telephone.

WHEN can a baby see clearly?　WHEN do bones break?

BABY'S SIGHT

Babies can generally see clearly by the time they are three to four months old. At birth they cannot focus on objects or control their eyes. Strong light upsets them.

After a month babies are able to focus on objects for a few moments at a time. After three months they can recognize things and follow their movements.

BROKEN BONES

Bones break under varying degrees of pressure according to age, health and other circumstances. They are made of hard, strong connective tissue and normally resist considerable force before breaking or fracturing. But when a bone has been softened by disease or grown fragile with age, fractures may follow very minor accidents or even occur spontaneously (pathological fractures).

The bones of children are not fully mature and are still relatively flexible. In childhood a severe blow or fall often results in a "greenstick" fracture, in which the bone appears to bend but does not completely break into two separate pieces.

An impacted fracture occurs when the broken ends of the bone appear to be jammed together by the force of the injury. A comminuted fracture is one in which the ends are shatted into many pieces. A fracture is called simple (closed) when the overlying skin is not broken, or compound (open) when the bone is exposed.

All fractures attempt to heal themselves by producing new tissue to join the broken pieces together. At first this tissue is like putty and easily injured. So, generally a fractured limb should be straightened, immobilized and protected by a plaster cast while the healing takes place. In time the new tissue, or fracture callus, changes into mature bone.

BLOOD TRANSFUSION

The first successful blood transfusion on record was performed in 1665 by Richard Lower. Using quills and silver tubes, he transferred the blood from the artery of one dog to the vein of another. Two years later, he transfused a man with the blood of a lamb. He gave a demonstration of this before

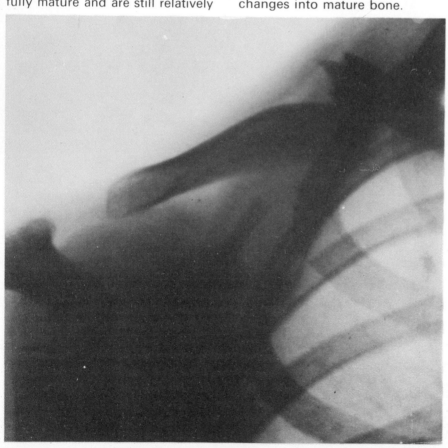

WHEN was the first blood transfusion?
WHEN was the thermometer invented?

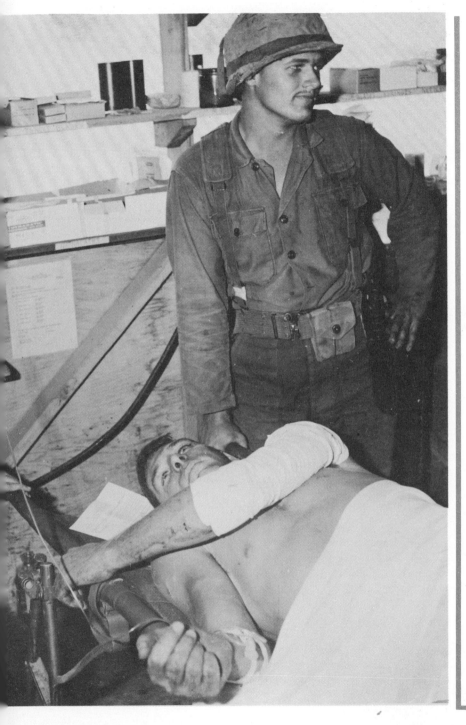

THERMOMETER

The first practical thermometer or instrument for measuring temperature was invented shortly before the end of the 16th Century by the famous Italian astronomer Galileo. It was an air thermometer giving only a rough indication of the degrees of heat and cold, and later he increased its efficiency by using alcohol instead of air.

The principle on which thermometers work is that the liquid or gas used for measuring expands or contracts with changes in temperature more rapidly than the glass containing it. Thus when a coloured liquid is confined in a thin glass tube the difference in expansion, as shown by the level of the liquid against a graduated scale, indicates the temperature.

About 1714 the German scientist Gabriel Daniel Fahrenheit designed a thermometer which, for the first time, used mercury as the measuring agent. He also introduced the scale named after him in which 32° is the freezing point of water and 212° the boiling point. Mercury is still used in most thermometers because it has a high boiling point (674°) and a low freezing point (−38°).

An alcohol thermometer, still in use in some countries, was made by René de Réaumur, a French naturalist, about 1731. About 11 years later Anders Celsius, a Swedish astronomer, used the centigrade scale for the first time, with freezing point at 0° and boiling point at 100°.

the Royal Society in London, and the incident is recorded in the diary of Samuel Pepys.

Richard Lower was able to perform these transfusions thanks to William Harvey who, in 1628, announced his theory of the circulation of the blood. Before Harvey, people had always realized that blood was vital to life, but they did not know how it circulated in the body.

A vital development in blood transfusion came in 1900, when Karl Landsteiner demonstrated the different blood groups in human beings. After that, people were transfused with blood of their own group whenever possible.

Nowadays blood transfusion saves many lives. People can be treated for shock by pumping plasma (the fluid part of the blood) into them. Large reserves of blood are necessary for open-heart operations, sometimes as much as 20 pints a patient.

CONGEALED BLOOD

Blood congeals when a part of the body is wounded. If it failed to congeal the injured person would die from loss of blood.

The congealing, or coagulation, of the blood, is the first step towards healing a wound. It closes the wound and builds a scaffold for new tissue by means of a chemical process in the plasma, the fluid part of the blood. In this process the platelets (small cellular bodies in the blood) produce thromboplastin. This changes fibronigin, a protein in the blood, into fibrin. Finally a spongy network of fibrin connects the edges of the wound and prevents the loss of any more blood cells. Often, a scab is formed over the wound as a protection.

ALBINOS

Albinos occur when there is an absence of yellow, red, brown or black pigments in an animal's eyes, skin, scales, feathers or hair. This peculiarity can be passed on from one generation to another. But albino animals do not often survive in the wild, because their normal colouring is designed to protect them against radiation or enemies.

In the case of human beings albinism is caused by the absence of the pigment melanin. It varies from complete albinism involving skin, hair and eyes, to localized albinism or spotting.

The complete human albino has milk-white skin and hair. The irises of his eyes appear pink, while his pupils take on a red hue from light reflected by blood in the unpigmented structures underneath. There is one complete albino for every 20,000 people.

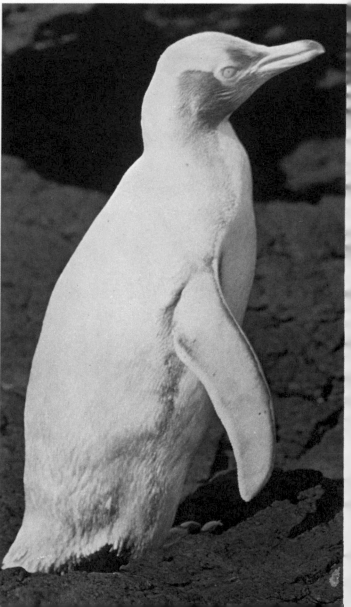

do people stop growing?

WHEN does the body produce adrenalin?

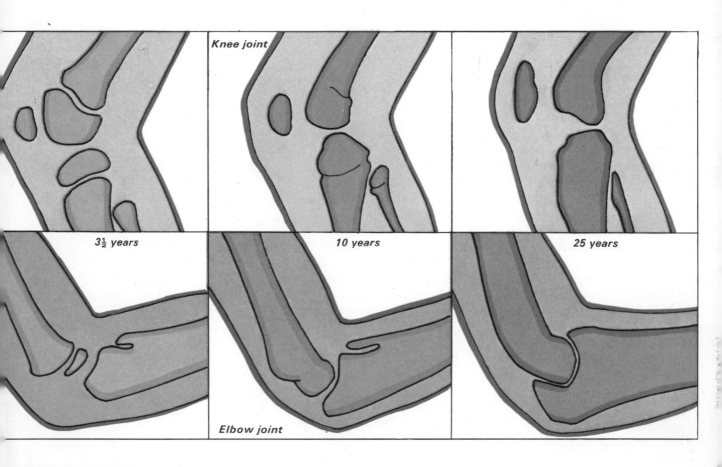

Knee joint

3½ years   10 years   25 years

Elbow joint

STOP GROWING

People stop growing when their bones do, and that is usually between 15 and 25 years of age.

Bones are made up of living tissue, composed of special cells which secrete round themselves material rich in calcium salts and as hard as marble. The formation of bone (ossification) is a complex process which usually begins in cartilage (gristle).

In a child the bone begins to form in the middle of the cartilage and spreads towards both ends, turning it all to bone with the exception of the tips. From these points the bone grows in length and so does the child. When the growing period is over the tips of the bones close by joining the main shaft of the bone.

Bones vary greatly in shape and size. Long ones act as levers. Flat ones are centres for muscle action. But each has a cavity containing bone marrow. Around this the bony substance is spongy in texture, becoming hard nearer the surface where the calcium is densest. On the surface of the bone is a special layer of fibrous tissue (the periosteum) which is rich in bone-building cells.

ADRENALIN

A person's body produces adrenalin when he is angry, frightened or challenged, or when he needs to be functioning at maximum efficiency to meet some sort of stress.

Adrenalin is a hormone, a substance which acts upon tissues and organs. It is secreted in the adrenal glands, which lie like a pair of pyramid-shaped caps, one on top of each kidney. Each gland has two parts, the outer shell, or cortex, and the inner core, or

medulla. The adrenal hormones come from the medulla and are released into the bloodstream.

They stimulate the liver both to release its sugar and to speed up its manufacture for muscular action. They also contract blood vessels, diverting blood from the skin and raising the pressure at which it is pumped through the brain and lungs and muscles. The heart and pulse quicken, the breathing speeds up, the body

heat rises and muscular fatigue is postponed. At the same time the ability of the blood to coagulate in the event of the person being wounded is increased.

This series of defence reactions occurs almost immediately. Adrenalin released by the glands is reinforced by more hormones produced at the sympathetic nerve ends. A hormone produced in the brain, called serotonin, stimulates the transmission of nerve impulses.

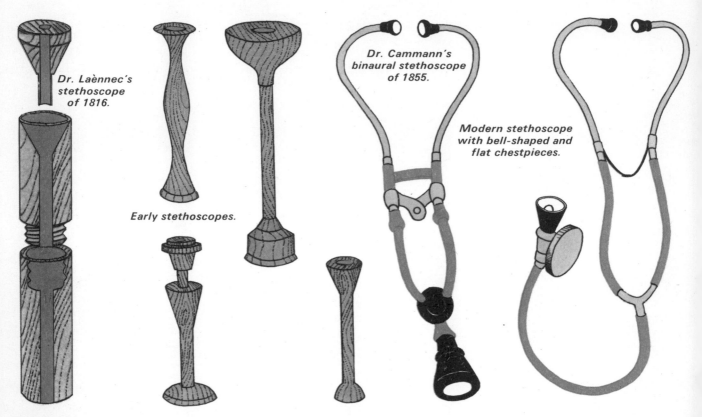

Dr. Laènnec's stethoscope of 1816.

Early stethoscopes.

Dr. Cammann's binaural stethoscope of 1855.

Modern stethoscope with bell-shaped and flat chestpieces.

STETHOSCOPE

The stethoscope was invented by a French doctor, René Théophile Hyacinthe Laënnec, in 1816. His stethoscope was a perforated wooden cylinder one foot long, and he got the idea for it from the sight of children scratching one end of a wooden beam with a pin and listening to the transmitted sound at the other end.

He put one end of the tube to his patient's chest and listened to noises made by the heart and lungs. He gathered evidence of what these sounds meant by comparing the various noises heard in living patients with the type of disease seen after they died. In 1819 he published his findings in one of the great books of medicine *De l'Auscultation Médiate*, and the stethoscope soon came into general use.

Auscultation (listening to sounds within the body) is most commonly used in diagnosing diseases of the heart and lungs. Nowadays a stethoscope is gener-ally binaural (for both ears) and has two flexible rubber tubes attaching the chestpiece to spring-connected metal tubes with ear-pieces. In listening it is often necessary to use both a bell-shaped, open-ended chestpiece for low-pitched sounds, and a flat chestpiece covered with a semi-rigid disc or diaphragm for high-pitched sounds. Many modern stethoscopes have both kinds of chestpieces, readily interchanged by turning a valve.

ULCERS

People get ulcers at various times, according to the kind of ulcers they are. Ulcers are wounds or breakages in the skin or tissues of the body.

The least serious are mouth ulcers. They usually arise from some minor infection, or through eating the wrong kinds of food. They are known as benign ulcers. People with varicose veins some-times get ulcers on their legs. This is because the blood in the skin is circulating too slowly.

If ulcers last for longer than a month, it may be because they are cancerous. These are known as malignant ulcers, and usually have hard edges. They can be dangerous if not discovered at once. The worst kind of ulcers are in the rectum. They cause pain, constipation and bleeding, and are difficult to remove if left long.

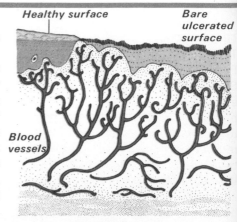

Healthy surface

Bare ulcerated surface

Blood vessels

lcers? **WHEN** was the iron lung invented?

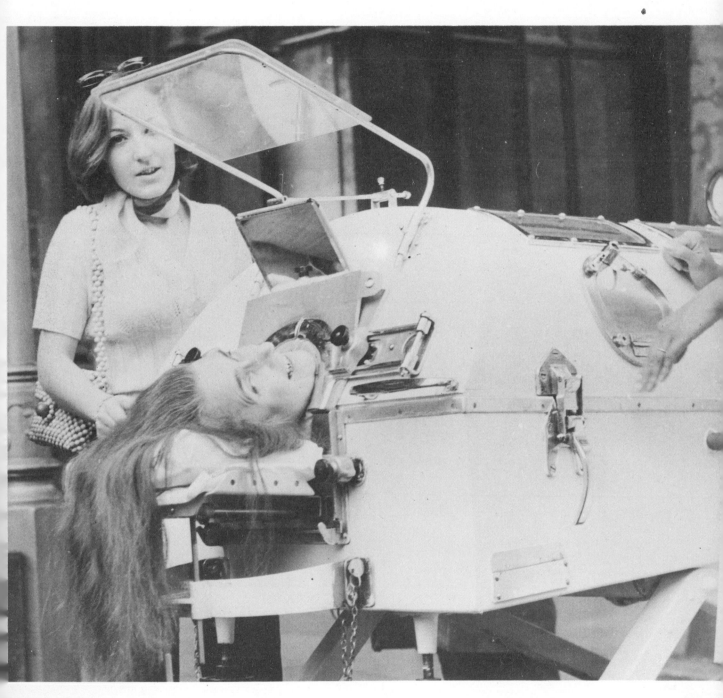

IRON LUNG

The iron lung was invented by Philip Drinker of Harvard, United States in 1929. This machine enables people whose lungs are paralysed by disease or accident to breathe. It does so by alternately reducing and increasing the air pressure round the patient's body. When the pressure is reduced, his chest expands and air streams into his lungs through the normal air passages in his head which is outside the machine. When the pressure is increased, the chest contracts and air is automatically expelled from the lungs.

This life-preserving apparatus is a tube on wheels in which the patient lies on a foam rubber bed with adjustable head and foot rests. It is operated by electricity, but has a safety device which gives a warning signal in the event of a power cut. The machine can then be operated by hand.

The cover on top of the iron lung can be opened to give access to the patient. When this is done, the patient's head is usually enclosed in a plastic dome in which the air pressure is alternately raised and lowered to enable breathing to continue.

WHEN does a heart attack happen? WHEN would yo

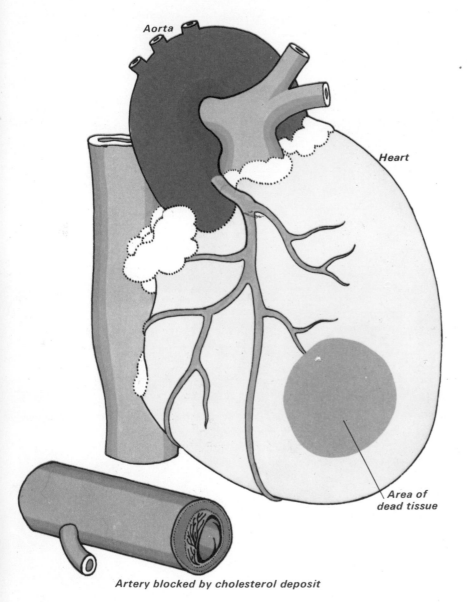

Aorta

Heart

Area of dead tissue

Artery blocked by cholesterol deposit

GALL STONES

Gall stones occur most often in women who are overweight and have had children, for in the late stages of pregnancy cholesterol, which makes up a large proportion of gall stones, is deposited in the liver in such quantities that the organ may not be able to take it all in. The liver also stores sugar, but overweight people usually take more sugar than they need. So once again the liver may not be able to cope.

Lying on the underside of the liver, the gall bladder drains the bile, stores it and then conveys it to the intestines. However, if the stones block the tube called the bile duct, or the gall bladder itself, severe pain will result. This is felt under the ribs on the right radiating up to the right shoulder, and lasts until the stone causing it passes out of the bile duct. If the stone is wedged, cholangitis or infection of the gall bladder may occur.

The treatment of cholelithiasis, or gall stones, usually necessitates an operation, for there is no known drug that can dissolve the stones. Drugs can be given to ease the pain and to relax the smooth muscles of the ducts. Often small stones cause more trouble than large ones, which stay in the gall bladder without emerging to block the bile ducts.

HEART ATTACK

A heart attack, clinically known as coronary thrombosis, occurs when the arteries leading to the heart are blocked by contraction, a blood clot or cholestrol. In either case the heart will not receive enough blood for it to function properly.

As a general rule the possibility of a heart attack increases with age. But many victims of heart attacks recover completely and go on to lead normal, healthy lives.

Heavy smoking greatly increases the risk of a heart attack. Sudden bouts of exercise in older people can also be risky.

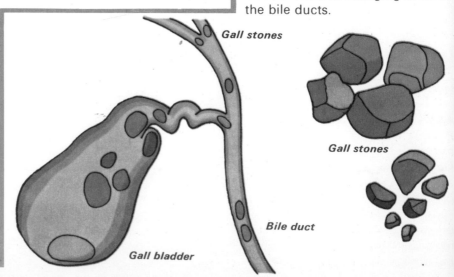

Gall stones

Gall stones

Bile duct

Gall bladder

6

xpect gall stones to occur? WHEN was aspirin first used?

Meadowsweet, one of the many plants which contain the ingredients for aspirin.

ASPIRIN

Aspirin was first introduced into medicine in 1899 by H. Dreser of Germany. The word aspirin is actually the trade name for a preparation of acetylsalicylic acid.

During the last century many preparations gall this acid were introduced for medical purposes, but Dreser was the first person to produce one which was considered satisfactory.

The main ingredients of aspirin occur naturally in the flowers, fruits, leaves and roots of many plants. South American Indians were familiar with the beneficial effects obtained from the bark of sweet birch and the leaves of the wintergreen shrub, which produce a medicine very similar to aspirin.

Aspirin is widely used for the treatment of headaches, sickness, colds and influenza. But too many aspirin tablets, instead of relieving the patient, may cause dizziness, headaches and sickness, and so they should be used carefully.

WHEN do people get hay fever?   WHEN does the brai

HAY FEVER

People get hay fever when they are allergic to small particles existing in the air. The most common causes are the pollens of certain plants. Therefore the hay fever seasons vary greatly in different parts of the world according to the vegetation present.

In North America ragweed is the worst offender, causing a great deal of distress in late summer and early fall. In Britain, pollen from timothy grass causes hay fever in spring and early summer.

Other causes are dust, animal hairs, moults and, of course, hay itself. Particles of these substances inflame the membranes of the sufferers' eyes and nose.

Temporary relief is sometimes obtained from antihistamine tablets which prevent a certain amount of inflammation in the nose. The most effective treatment is immunization by a series of injections of pollen extract. Many sufferers get relief from this.

Timothy Grass.

Loading a haycart.

BRAIN DECLINE

The brain begins to show signs of decline after a certain proportion of the nerve cells or neurons of which it is formed have died. The age at which this happens varies.

A grown man has no more nerve cells than he did when he was born. These cells do not multiply as the body grows, as bone and skin cells do. Indeed, as a person grows older he has fewer and fewer nerve cells, because those destroyed are not replaced.

At the age of 70 or 80, as many as a quarter of the nerve cells may have died. That is the reason some old people cannot hear well or have poor memories. Yet others manage to retain their faculties and abilities until they are very old. Recent techniques have made it easier for scientists to study how our brains function, but there is still a great deal to discover.

BLOOD-LETTING

Blood-letting was a common form of medical treatment from before the time of Hippocrates (400 B.C.), the Greek "father of medicine" and was still much in fashion for various ailments a century ago. A bleeding-glass formed part of the symbol of the physician in ancient Egypt.

The old ideas about blood-letting, or phlebotomy, arose from a theory that certain body fluids, known as "humours", controlled a person's illnesses and decided his character. Today we call a person "sanguine" if he is optimistic or cheerful, but to a doctor in the Middle Ages a sanguine man was one in whom hot blood predominated over his other humours. A "phlegmatic" or stolid man was one who suffered from too much cold, wet phlegm.

For many illnesses it was considered that the best cure was to restore the balance of humours by relieving the body of diseased blood. Bleeding became almost a panacea, a cure-all. Monks were bled regularly to keep their minds from worldly thoughts. Madame de Maintenon (1635–1719) was said to have been bled to stop her from blushing.

Blood-letting was prescribed by doctors, but performed by barbers. The barbers took over as surgeons in 1163, when a papal decree forbade the clergy to shed blood, and they continued the profession for six centuries. On a barber's pole the red stripes represent the blood and the white ones the bandages, while the gilt knob at the end is the symbol of the basin in which the barber-surgeon caught the blood—or the lather.

In the 19th Century many people still had themselves bled regularly as a treatment for various illnesses, especially those due to over indulgence in food and drink. Frequently people did not from the disease but from the supposed cure. Blood-sucking worms called leeches were often used, being regarded as an essential part of a doctor's equipment.

Even today the withdrawal of blood is said to help certain conditions, and leeches are still used in some countries, particularly in the East.

4

WHEN is a Caesarean operation necessary?

WHEN were contact lense

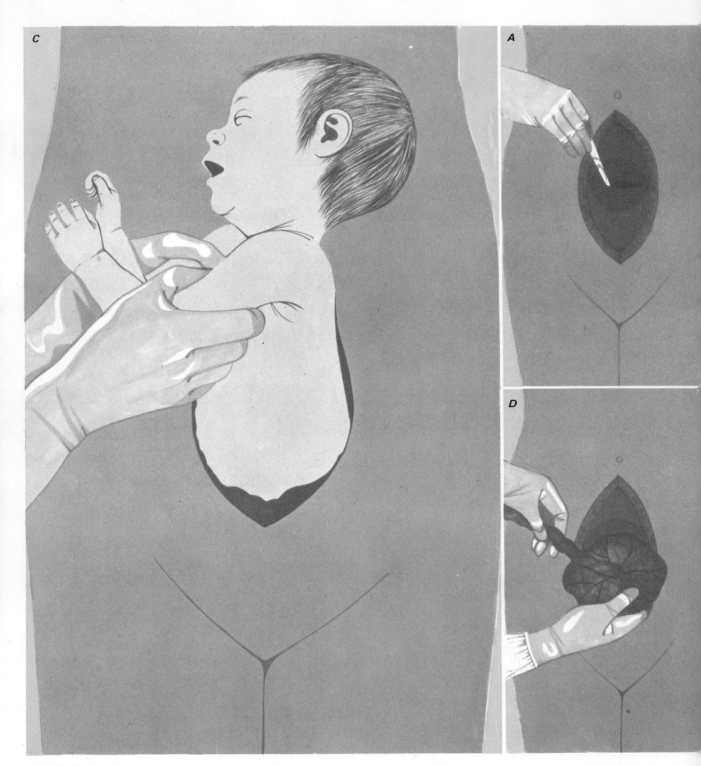

CAESAREAN

A Caesarean operation is necessary for the surgical delivery of a baby when a natural childbirth is difficult or impossible. The surgeon makes an incision into the mother's abdomen and delivers the baby through the wall of the womb.

The operation owes its name to the belief that Julius Caesar was born by this means. Deliveries of this kind were certainly known in ancient times. They are even mentioned in the Jewish law book, the Talmud, which dates back

some two thousand years.

In the 19th Century, three-quarters of those who underwent such an operation died due to primitive techniques. Now they are nearly always completely successful.

nvented? WHEN is it dangerous for a male to have mumps?

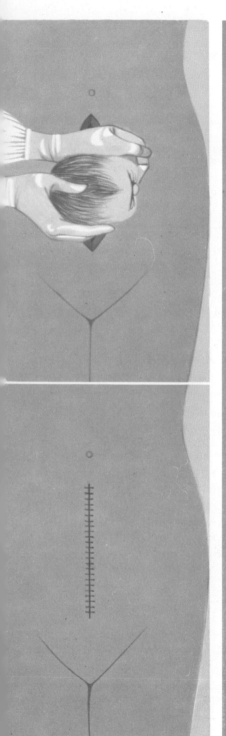

This is one kind of Caesarean operation A An incision is made in the abdomen B The baby's head is helped out first C Then the body is eased out D The placenta, or after-birth, is taken away E The abdomen is sewn up again

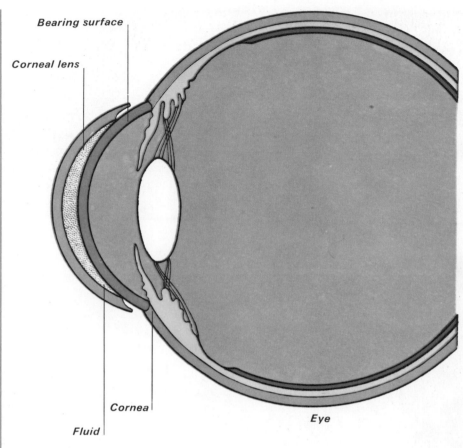

Bearing surface

Corneal lens

Cornea

Fluid

Eye

CONTACT LENSES

The first contact lenses were made by A. E. Fick in 1887, but were not successful. During the early part of this century opticians tried to produce extremely thin shell-like lenses to fit closely over the eye. An impression was taken of the eye and a glass shell made which, with a suitable fluid under it, covered most of the eye. After 1938, plastic was used instead of glass, and about 1950 smaller lenses were introduced which covered only the cornea and floated on a layer of tears. These lenses, only 7 to 11 millimetres in diameter and 0·1 to 1 mm thick can usually be worn all day without being removed.

Besides being invisible, contact lenses provide a much wider field of vision than spectacles. They are more practical for use in active sports because they are not easily lost or broken, and they can be tinted for use as sunglasses. But contact lenses are not effective in all cases of eye trouble. They are also expensive, and some people find difficulty in learning to wear them.

As research continues, even smaller and more flexible lenses are being developed.

MUMPS IN MALES

Mumps can be dangerous for a male after the age of puberty, because the illness can affect the testicles and, in severe cases, cause sterility.

Mumps is a virus infection and it is rare to have more than one attack. The parotid glands in the neck swell and opening or shutting the mouth can be painful. It is possible that only one side of the neck is affected.

WHEN was penicillin discovered? WHEN was ths firs
WHEN can electric shocks help to cure people?

PENICILLIN

Penicillin was discovered in 1929 by Sir Alexander Fleming, then a professor and lecturer at the Royal College of Surgeons in London. He wanted to find a substance which would kill bacteria but would not also poison the tissues of the patient's body.

Fleming discovered penicillin by accident while he was researching into influenza. He was examining a staphylococcus, a kind of germ, when he noticed that it had created a bacteria-free circle of mould around itself. When he experimented further, he discovered that this liquid mould, which he named penicillin, prevented further growth of the staphylococcus germ even when diluted and made 80 times weaker. Also, penicillin had no poisonous effect on the human cells.

Sir Alexander Fleming published his results in the *Journal of Experimental Pathology* in 1929.

For some time it was thought that there was only one penicillin, but later it was discovered that the mould could produce four penicillins. They were distinguished by the letters F, G, X and K. The best known is penicillin G, which came into widespread use after the Second World War.

HEART TRANSPLANT

The first human heart transplant took place on December 3, 1967 at Groote Schuur Hospital, Cape Town, South Africa. A team of 20 surgeons, headed by Dr Christiaan Barnard, operated on Louis Washkansky, aged 55, using the heart of a 24-year-old donor, Denise Ann Darvall, who had been killed in a road accident.

Both the donor and the recipient were of the same blood group and the heart was kept in cooled oxygenated blood for more than three hours before transplantation. The operation took five hours and the new heart was only half the size of Washkansky's. The operation itself was a success, and within a few days Washkansky was sitting up, eating and talking happily. The doctors were anxious about transplant rejection by the body and also post-operative infection which, in fact, did kill Washkansky within a month of the transplant.

In January 1968 a second transplant was carried out on Philip Blaiberg, a 58-year-old dentist, who subsequently overcame a severe liver infection and lung condition, thought to be the result of his body trying to reject the new heart. By the end of 1968 more than 100 transplants had been carried out in the United States, Britain, France, India, South America, Canada, Czechoslovakia and Israel. More than 40 patients survived. Blaiberg remained alive until August 17, 1969 and other patients survived for up to two and a half years, but the number of operations declined. From December 1970 to May 1971 only six operations were performed. Caution took the place of optimism uman heart transplant?

WHEN were antiseptics first used?

ELECTRIC SHOCKS

Electric shock treatment, or electro-convulsive therapy, is sometimes used with people suffering from mental illnesses in which severe depression is the main symptom.

It was first used in 1938 by U. Cerletti and L. Bini in Rome, and was recommended for the treatment of manic-depression and schizophrenia (literally, "splitting of the mind").

The technique of electrocon-vulsive therapy is to place two electrodes on the temples of the patient and pass alternating currents through his head. This causes him to lose consciousness immediately and is followed by a convulsion of the body. It is claimed that the patient is much calmer and better-balanced when he regains consciousness. In general, treatment is given three times a week for periods from two to six weeks. Some acutely disturbed patients, however, have been given as many as two or three treatments in a day.

This treatment has become less common since the discovery of tranquillizing drugs which reduce feelings of anxiety and agitation without too many side-effects.

Weak electrical shocks are also used in physiotherapy to stimulate muscles wasted by disease.

ANTISEPTICS

Antiseptics were first used in 1865 by a surgeon called Joseph Lister, in London. He was helped by his knowledge of the work of Louis Pasteur, a French doctor, who had discovered that putrefaction (rotting), was caused by live bacteria and not by a chemical process.

Lister, shown above, thought that bacteria could be destroyed before they entered a wound and poisoned it. He first tried the treatment on a compound fracture. Carbolic acid was applied to the wound in the hope that this would provide a barrier against the germs in the atmosphere. The experiment was successful and led to a great advance in surgery. Various kinds of antiseptics came into general use to combat bacteria.

Geography and the Earth

PANAMA CANAL

The Panama Canal was finally opened on August 15, 1914. It had taken ten years to build. At first much delay was caused by uncertainty over the type of canal that should be built. Some experts contemplated a high-level canal with locks at either end, while others suggested a canal at sea level. After two years the high-level plan was adopted. It was decided that the alternative system would threaten the land on either side of the canal with flooding and also put ships at risk in stormy weather.

The building of the Panama Canal, one of the great engineering feats in the world, was masterminded by John F. Stevens. The canal zone was formally acquired by the United States from Panama in 1904 for 10 million dollars plus an annual payment of 250,000 dollars. The United States was to be responsible for the construction of the canal and for its perpetual maintenance, sanitation, operation and defence. Since that date the treaty has been amended several times.

Since 1904 the canal, which is just over 40 miles long, has cost the United States well over 6,000 million dollars. But it has shortened the distance for ships travelling between that country's Atlantic and Pacific coasts by 8,000 miles. Ships going from Europe to Australia make a saving of nearly 2,000 miles.

Among the canal's many engineering marvels, its great locks attract particular attention. They are deep enough to take vessels drawing forty feet of water and have a length of 1,000 feet. Some of the "leaves" of the lock weigh as much as 730 tons and are more than 80 feet high.

PEAT

Peat bogs are formed in mild and humid climates when the land drainage is so bad that pools of water submerge masses of partially decomposed vegetable matter and prevent complete decay.

After being dug out of the bog, the peat is left to try in the open air. When the water has evaporated it will burn readily. Vast quantities of peat exist in many parts of Europe, North America and northern Asia, but it is normally used as a fuel only in countries or regions where there is little coal. Large quantities are used for fires and ovens in Ireland, Scandinavia and the Soviet Union.

WHEN does an atoll take shape?

ATOLL

An atoll or coral reef begins to form when tiny marine animals called coral polyps attach themselves to rocks on the sea bed. The reef, which eventually takes the shape of a ring or horseshoe enclosing a lagoon, is made up of the lime-based skeletons of innumerable polyps.

After building skeletons round themselves, coral polyps produce new polyps, which in turn surround themselves with skeletons. The young polyps remain attached to the parents so that succeeding generations combine to produce a great mass of coral.

Atolls occur only in shallow water where the temperature is over 65° Fahrenheit (18·3° Centigrade). They are found in the West Indies, the Indian Ocean, along the coast of Brazil and, notably, in the Pacific. North-east of Australia huge reefs have formed and some atolls may stretch 40 miles in diameter and more than a thousand feet in depth.

WHEN do glaciers move? WHEN were the Ice Ages? WHEN was the eocen

GLACIERS

A glacier moves when the pressure above it from rocks, loose ice and snow becomes greater than the strength of the ice. Under this enormous weight, the solid ice tends to flow like tar, although very slowly. The glacier must be quite old before enough material accumulates to exert the pressure needed to move it—usually when it is about 60 feet thick.

The movement of glaciers is too slow to be noticed by the eye, but measurements have shown they may travel as much as 150 feet a day. The bodies of mountaineers buried by avalanches have been carried several miles in a few years.

Glaciers cover 10 per cent of the earth's land surface.

The movement of the great glaciers is too slow to be measured by eye.

ICE AGES

The Ice Ages ended about 10,000 years ago after lasting about two million years. At its greatest extent the ice covered nearly 30 per cent of the land surface of the world, compared with about 10 per cent today. The great glaciers reached as far south in America as present-day Nebraska and Kansas and extended over the whole of northern Europe down to a line linking London and Berlin.

But there were a number of intervals when temperatures rose and the ice retreated temporarily to its present limits. During these warm periods, which totalled several hundred years, the liberated areas were repopulated. The climate is believed to have been warmer at times than it is today.

MOHS' SCALE

Mohs' scale is used to measure the hardness of substances. The scale was introduced by the German mineralogist Friedrich Mohs in 1812. It is based on a classification of 10 minerals. These are arranged in a table so that each of them is hard enough to scratch those below it, but not hard enough to scratch any of those above it.

The scale in order of decreasing hardness is: 10, diamond; 9, carborundum and sapphire; 8, topaz; 7, quartz; 6, orthoclase; 5, apatite; 4, fluorite; 3, calcite; 2, gypsum; 1, talc. The divisions are, however, not equal. For instance, on an abolute scale, the difference in hardness between 10 (diamond) and 9 (carborundum) is four times greater than the difference between 9 (carborundum) and 1 (talc).

The 10 minerals thus provide a table of reference, against which the comparative hardness of other minerals can be measured.

EOCENE PERIOD

The eocene geological period began about 55 million years ago, and lasted between 15 million and 17 million years. During this period animals, fishes and plants made enormous evolutionary progress, in some cases coming very close to those familiar today.

During the eocene period the climate got warmer, and many plants became extinct. But new plants, especially flowering varieties, evolved, giving the world's vegetation a more modern appearance.

On land many familiar mammals appeared to replace more primitive animals now dying out. Horses were abundant, there were also tapirs and rhinoceroses. Pigs and camels began to appear but increased only slowly, because of constant attacks from the now extinct sabre-toothed tigers.

GREEN REVOLUTION

The increase in agricultural production throughout the world since 1945 has been so great it has come to be known as the Green Revolution.

World agricultural production in 1964 was one and a half times that of 1948. Much of this increase was due to the redistribution of land and to the grouping of small holdings into larger units.

Scientists have contributed new varieties of grass that provide better cover and strength, thus holding the soil in place. Advances have been made in the development of new kinds of plants capable of withstanding drought and maturing fast enough to avoid freezing. Research has led to the discovery of new production methods, fertilizers and pesticides.

Dawn horse or eochippus, Hyracotherium

Dinocerate Uintatherium

Phenacodus

WHEN does an underground river form?   WHEN will the

UNDERGROUND RIVER

An underground river is formed when the top soil of the land makes it extremely easy for water to pass through to a more solid soil structure. Another kind of underground river is created when a powerful spring in a mountain has to find a channel to the surface owing to the solidity and compactness of the rocks.

Finally, an underground river may form as an effluent to a larger river above ground, if there are faults in the surrounding land.

Some rivers travel underground only for a part of the journey, such as the Rhône in France.

An underground river at Wookey Hole, in Somerset, England.

WORLD'S OIL

Many experts believe that the world's oil supply may run out by the end of the century unless vast new oil fields are discovered.

At the end of 1969 the total known reserves of crude oil were calculated at more than 500,000 million barrels, or 21,000,000 million gallons. At the present consumption rate of 50 million barrels a day, this supply would run out in around 30 years from now. However, it has been estimated that consumption will be more than 80 million barrels a day by 1980 and more than 120 million barrels a day by the year 2000.

But by then more efficient methods may have been invented for getting the maximum amount of oil out of the ground. Also, extensive new deposits may have been found, possibly in Antarctica or under the sea, on a much bigger scale than the discoveries off the coasts of Britain and northern Europe.

The possibilities of producing oil from shale on a commercial scale are now being investigated in the United States.

GEYSER

A geyser occurs when a hot spring erupts, hurling a column of water and steam high into the air. These springs are situated in regions which were formerly volcanic and which have retained considerable heat near the surface.

They usually have craters with well-like shafts penetrating into the earth. The water which gathers deep down in these shafts becomes heated until the lower part is changed into steam. The pressure of the steam steadily mounts to a point when it suddenly hurls the water above it into the air, sometimes to a height of over 100 feet.

The chief geyser districts are in Iceland (home of the Great Geyser), in the Yellowstone National Park, Wyoming, United States, and in New Zealand. For four years Waimangu in New Zealand, the greatest of all geysers, was capable of spouting jets up to 1,500 feet.

RIFT VALLEY

The great rift valleys of the earth took shape during the pleistocene age, about two million years ago. They were caused mainly by volcanic eruptions powerful enough to split a mountain range, thus creating a rift between the two sides of the volcano.

Rift valleys are to be found in all parts of the world where volcanic action has been common. The most impressive example is the Great Rift Valley which extends from Jordan in south-west Asia to Mozambique in southern Africa. Many big lakes are situated within the valley's boundaries.

Extremely steep edges are characteristic of these valleys. In Africa their valleys rise to heights of 10,000 feet on either side.

CLAY

Clay is formed from earth and various minerals as a result of weather conditions such as heat and rain. Occasionally clay is produced by processes dependant on hot underground springs.

Wet clay has much the same constituency as a soft plastic and is capable of containing water.

When dry, clay becomes hard and takes on a permanent shape.

No other material on earth can be used in so many different ways. Clay provides the mechanical and chemical environment for almost all plant life and, therefore, can be said to support all the life on earth.

Once extracted from the soil, clays are used in a wide variety of industries, including engineering, paper making, brick making, cement and chemicals. The use of clay in pottery predates recorded history, and it has largely been due to pottery finds that archaeologists have been able to analyse and record past civilizations.

A quarry of Carrara marble in North-West Tuscany, Italy.

SEXTANT

The sextant was invented in England in 1731 by John Hadley. Hadley's instrument is used mainly at sea to determine a ship's latitude, or distance from the Equator. Its invention laid the foundation of modern navigation with the aid of the sun and stars.

The instrument is so called because it is equipped with an arc which is usually one-sixth of a circle, or 60 degrees. It measures the angle of the sun's or a star's altitude above the horizon. As this angle varies with the distance from the Equator, the information obtained helps the navigator to calculate his position. All he needs in addition is the time, the date and the longitude which can be found by comparing local time with the time at Greenwich.

To operate the sextant, the navigator looks through its small telescope straight at the horizon. At the same time, an image of the sun is reflected by mirrors into the user's field of vision. When the sun is made to appear exactly on the horizon, the arm which moves the mirrors gives the required measurements to calculate the ship's position.

The handling of a sextant is generally referred to as "shooting the sun".

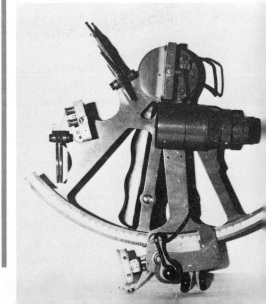

MARBLE

Marble is formed when granular limestone or dolomite rocks crystallize twice under the influence of heat, pressure, liquids and chemical action. These rocks undergo what is known as metamorphism, a complete change from one state to another.

Most of the marble existing today was formed many millions of years ago and is usually quarried from deep under the earth. It is used for buildings and monuments, sculpture and table tops. The chief discoveries of marble have been made in Italy (Carrara marble), Mexico, the United States (onyx), Norway and Greece.

WHEN is a forest called a rain forest?

When does sheet lightning occur?

RAIN FOREST

Rain forests are so-called because they grow in the wet lowlands of the tropics where the annual rainfall is more than 80 inches (2,000 mm) and the average temperature is between 20° and 30° Centigrade (65° and 85° Fahrenheit).

They consist of evergreen trees which never completely loose their luxurious leaves and grow over 100 feet high. Although it is possible to find as many as 100 different kinds of trees in a small area, most of them are similar.

Contrary to popular belief the rain forest is not a jungle. In most cases there is little vegetation apart from the trees and few flowers. This is because the tops of the trees are so dense that little sunlight reaches the ground.

Those plants that do grow beneath the tree line are mostly climbers winding their way up the barks of trees and such flowers as are found are usually the most exotic varieties on earth.

SHEET LIGHTNING

Sheet lightning usually occurs during a storm as the result of a discharge of excess electricity within a single thundercloud. The outline is obscured and the result is a diffused light spread over a large area of the sky in contrast to the vivid spiral or ribbon-like flashes of chain, forked or zig-zag lightning. The most favourable conditions for sheet lightning are provided when the electric field is equal throughout the area. Unlike other forms of lightning it does not reach the ground and the channel cannot be distinguished.

What is often referred to as sheet lightning is merely the lighting up of the sky by flashes occurring beyond the horizon.

All lightning is the natural discharge of large accumulations of electric charges in the atmosphere. It may take place between neigh-

Fork lightning taken with a five-minute exposure at night on Agfacolourfilm.

bouring clouds or between cloud and earth. Just before the discharge the cloud's electric poten-

tial is often built up by the action of falling raindrops or other natural processes.

WHEN does coal become a precious stone?

PRECIOUS COAL

Coal is basically a compound consisting largely of carbon. When a piece of carbon deep underground is subjected to great heat and pressure, it may gradually be transformed into a diamond. The heat turns the carbon into a liquid and the pressure causes it to crystallize.

Thus the carbon loses its black unattractive appearance and becomes the most precious of stones.

It has been calculated that this extraordinary process takes place at least 75 miles beneath the earth's surface, the diamonds being afterwards transported upwards by natural forces.

Some iron meteorites full of carbon have been found to contain diamonds deep inside. Here the heat and pressure conditions would be much the same as those formed underground.

Much the same conditions are created in the laboratory to make synthetic diamonds for industrial purposes, such as cutting hard materials. Only industrial diamonds are man-made. The diamonds that are considered the most precious stones in the world took thousands of years to form.

WHEN is pumice stone formed? WHEN will man be able t

WHEN was coffee first grown? WHEN are contou

PUMICE STONE

Pumice stone is formed when molten volcanic glass, ejected from beneath the earth's crust, cools so rapidly that there is no time for it to crystalize.

After the pumice has solidified, the gases inside are suddenly released and the stone swells up into its characteristic light and airy form. If the substance had cooled under greater pressure it would have turned into solid glass.

The stones have long been used for cleaning and polishing. Since the Second World War it has been employed widely in railroad building, masonry and insulation. Good pumice is found in Iceland, the Canaries, New Zealand, Greece, the Pacific coast of the United States and many other areas with a volcanic background.

WEATHER CONTROL

Since the 1940s scientists have discovered techniques by which several weather conditions can be controlled. For example, it is possible to prevent lightning by using an electrical earth to diffuse the electrical content of a cloud. The American scientist V. J. Schaefer has shown that it is feasible to produce greater concentrations of ice in clouds than occur under normal conditions.

Weather experts already are taking advantage of these discoveries to increase snowfall on mountains for winter sports, to prevent damaging hailstones and to moderate, or even prevent, the development of dangerous storms. Scientists are now able, in some cases, to make a cloud burst to produce rainfall over parched areas.

These local efforts may lead the way to large-scale weather control. But before then scientists may have to learn to cope with the damaging effect of air pollution on weather conditions.

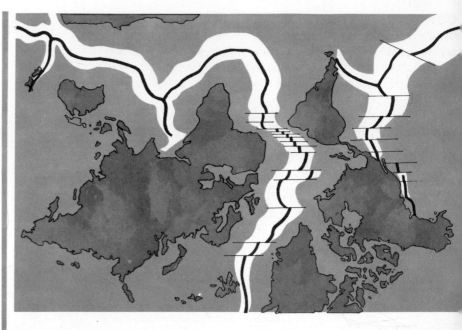

OCEAN MAPS

The shape of the ocean floor was not accurately determined until the 1920s. Until the end of the last century mapping had depended on the accounts by sailors of rock formations and deep troughs in the ocean bed.

Recent scientific developments, and new instruments and techniques have enabled maps to be drawn with greater accuracy and detail. By transmitting sound waves from ships to the sea bed, and back, it is possible to make a record of the changes in depth.

Mechanical, acoustical and electronic instruments have pictured the ocean floor not as a vast plain but as a series of mountain ranges, valleys, peaks and canyons. Some of the mountains are far higher than most of those on land and the deepest part of the ocean is much farther below sea level than the highest land mountain is above it.

COFFEE

A legend says the coffee plant first grew in Kaffa, a province in south Ethiopia, where it was discovered by a goatherd called Kaldi about the year 850. Kaldi's goats were reported to have skipped and pranced in a strange manner after feeding on an evergreen plant. The goatherd, so the story goes, tried some of the berries himself and excitedly dashed to the nearest town to tell of his find, which was called coffee after the name of the province.

Another theory is that the word coffee is probably derived from the Arabic *qahwah*. Certainly coffee was introduced into Europe from Arabia during the 16th and 17th Centuries. The first licence to sell coffee in the United States was issued to Dorothy Jones of Boston in 1670. The coffee houses of this time became famous meeting places for discussion.

As the drinking of coffee became more popular, its production spread to Java, Haiti, Dutch Guiana, Brazil, Cuba, Jamaica, Puerto Rica, Costa Rica, Venezuela, Mexico, Colombia, the Hawaiian Islands and, in this century, Africa.

Right: *coffee beans drying in the sun in a small Guinea village*.

ontrol the weather? WHEN was the ocean floor first mapped?

nes used on maps?

CONTOUR LINES

Contour lines are used when maps are designed to show the physical nature of the land. They do this by linking all points which are the same height above sea level. The width between the contour lines indicates the steepness of gra-dients or slopes in the area. The closer the lines are together, the steeper is the slope.

On physical maps giving the height of mountains, rivers, lakes and principal towns all areas between certain heights are gener-ally shown in the same colour. This is known as layer colouring.

Other methods for indicating heights include relief maps moulded in plastic to the physical feature raised as on a model. Spot heights may be shown, but these merely give the heights above sea level of certain points of the map and it does not follow that the ground rises evenly from one point to another.

Very old maps have mountains drawn on them. Later ones have lines called hachures radiating from a central point, with longer lines to show gentler slopes. Another system is to show the form of the land by hill shading. But none of these methods is so effective as the use of contour lines.

Thick line shows axial rift valley; white shows oceanic trenches.

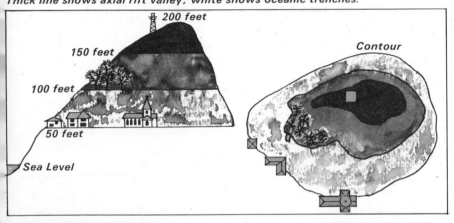

Science and Technology

NEON SIGN

The first neon sign was made by Georges Claude in France in 1910. Neon, an inert gas, was discovered in 1898 by the British scientists Sir William Ramsay and M. W. Travers. It is colourless, odourless and tasteless and is widely distributed in nature. Neon is called an inert gas because it is not affected by the usual chemical reactions.

In 1850 a German physicist, Heinrich Gessler, demonstrated that a brilliant light is produced when electricity is discharged through such a gas. Neon proved to be ideal for advertising because of its unusually high electrical conductivity, its adaptibility, its high luminosity and the brilliant colours obtainable by the addition of other inert gases and mercury vapour.

But neon light tubes do not give enough light for general illumination, and the colours that can be produced from it are not suitable for indoor lighting.

LITMUS PAPER

Litmus paper turns red when placed in an acid solution, but blue if the solution is alkaline. This absorbent paper is the oldest and most commonly used indicator of the presence or absence of acid. Its special qualities are due to the fact that it has been soaked and impregnated with a mixture of dyes called litmus.

The litmus mixture was originally produced by the action of air, ammonia and an alkali carbonate on certain lichens found in the Netherlands. It is now made from azolitmin and erythrolitmin.

A litmus solution is sometimes used. But the message is the same. A few drops added to a liquid turns it red if acid and blue if alkaline.

MAN ON A PLANET

No definite date can be given for man's first landing on another planet, but it is not expected until after the next decade. The first planet to be visited is likely to be Mars. Venus, the nearest to earth, is too inhospitable, for it is enveloped in gases and has a surface temperature of about 900° Centigrade (1,650° Fahrenheit).

Already much effort has been devoted to finding out the conditions which would have to be overcome on a planetary journey. The Russians have organized "sampler" expeditions with unmanned, radio-controlled space vehicles. At the same time Americans aboard the "sky laboratory" in orbit round the earth have concentrated on the problems of enduring long periods of space travel.

nother planet? WHEN was the first neon sign made?

WHEN was the telephone invented? WHEN was the firs

TELEPHONE

Alexander Graham Bell (1847–1922) invented and patented in 1876 the first telephone that was of any real practical use. In 1874 he said: "If I could make a current of electricity vary in intensity precisely as the air varies in density during the production of sound, I should be able to transmit speech telegraphically." This is the principle of the telephone.

On March 10, 1876, the first historic message was telephoned to Thomas A. Watson, Bell's assistant, who was in another room: "Mr Watson, come here; I want you."

Bell's first machine gave electrical currents too feeble to be of much use for the general public. In 1877 the American scientist Thomas A. Edison (1847–1931) invented the variable-contact carbon transmitter, which greatly increased the power of the signals.

The telephone was immediately popular in the United States, but Bell found little interest in Britain when he visited the country in 1878. Then Queen Victoria asked for a pair of telephones and the royal interest resulted in a London telephone exchange being formed in 1879 with eight subscribers

Bell inaugurating the New York–Chicago telephone line, October 1892

ristwatch made ? WHEN is Halley's comet next expected ?

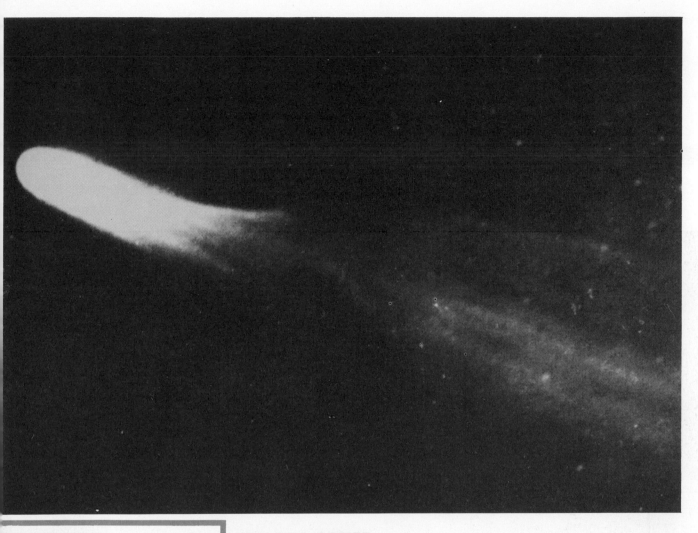

WRISTWATCH

The exact time the first wristwatch appeared is not known. But soon after the beginning of the 20th Century women's small pocket watches began to be fitted into specially made leather or gold adaptors to be worn on the wrist. They were immediately successful, and their popularity rapidly increased in the First World War because they could be consulted without undoing a coat or uniform jacket.

The first self-winding wristwatch was invented by John Harwood, an Englishman who patented it in 1924. Today the largest watchmaking industry in the world is concentrated in the Jura mountains and the valley of the Aar in Switzerland.

HALLEY'S COMET

Halley's Comet is next expected to appear in 1986. It is the most famous of all periodical comets— those which move round the sun and reappear in our skies at known intervals.

The comet is named after the British astronomer, Edmund Halley (1656–1742) who observed it in 1682. He predicted accurately that it would return in 1758, but died too soon to see it. Halley's Comet has a period of 76 years and was last seen in 1910, when this photograph was taken.

Comets have been called the stray members of the solar system, but the description is misleading as a comet's orbit can be calculated like that of a planet, though they may appear unexpectedly.

A comet is formed of relatively small particles contained in an envelope of thin gas. A large comet has a concentrated head or nucleus, from which streams a long, brilliant tail, but a small one may have no tail. Although a comet may be larger than the earth or even Jupiter, it contains only a small quantity of matter. This lack of substance makes it invisible until relatively close to the earth.

A comet's tail always points away from the sun, probably because of the intense radiation which repels the tail's tiny particles. Its orbit is much more elliptical than that of a planet, and, because they are so insubstantial, they can be seen only when relatively near the Earth.

WHEN is the best time to launch a rocket to the moon?

ROCKET LAUNCH

There is virtually no "best time" to launch a rocket to the moon, because, in terms of space travel, the journey is so short. The average distance is 238,000 miles, with a maximum variation of only 25,000 miles.

A space shot, whether to the moon or some other object, is made by a rocket already in orbit. To take a rocket out of orbit and put it on course for the moon calls for a boost in speed to 25,000 miles (40,000 kilometres) an hour. This is necessary to overcome the pull of the earth's gravity. The moment when the engines are refired to start the rocket on its journey does not depend on the position of the launching base in relation to the rocket or the moon.

In contrast, the great variations in the distances between the earth and Mars or Venus make the launching of a rocket to the planets impractical for periods of nine to eighteen months.

WHEN were dish telescopes first used?

DISH TELESCOPES

The first dish (or radio) telescope was made in 1942 by an American, Grote Reber, of Wheaton, Illinois. He constructed his apparatus after studying the experiments of K. G. Jansky, another American. Jansky discovered in 1935 that the intensity of radiowaves increases as a highly sensitive aerial is directed progressively nearer to the Milky Way. The maximum intensity is reached when the antenna is pointing towards Sagittarius—that is to say, towards the galactic centre.

Radio telescopes are called dish telescopes because of the steerable dish-shaped or parabolic reflector which gathers the radiation and focuses it on to a centrally mounted aerial. The surface of the dish is made of a good electrical conductor and the radio waves are reflected from it. The parabaloid shape ensures that all the reflected rays arrive at the central point, where they are "swallowed" by an electromagnetic horn and fed into a receiver.

Since the Second World War the development of radio telescopes has gone ahead rapidly. A 250-foot diameter instrument was installed at the Nuffield Radio Astronomy Laboratories at Jodrell Bank, Cheshire, England. It is under the direction of Professor Sir Bernard Lovell and has already contributed a great deal of new information to astronomy.

WHEN was the first supersonic flight? WHEN did talkin

This is the Bell X-1A, which succeeded the Bell X-1. In 1953, Yeager flew at 1,600 m.p.h. in the Bell X-1A.

SUPERSONIC FLIGHT

The first time a manned aircraft exceeded the speed of sound (Mach 1) on a level flight was on October 14, 1947. Captain Charles E. Yeager of the United States Air Force flew America's Bell X-1 rocket-propelled research aircraft 42,000 feet over Edwards Air Force Base, Muroc, California, at a speed of Mach 1·015 (670 miles an hour).

Known as Glamorous Glennis, this aircraft was the first rocket-propelled aircraft in the world designed for research into high speed aerodynamics. It was a single-seater monoplane with an enclosed pressurized cabin lying flush to the surface.

In 1946 the X-1 underwent a series of tests during which it was released from a Boeing B-29 Superfortress in flight and allowed to glide to earth. The aircraft first flew under its own power after one such drop on December 9, 1946. But its first take-off under power did not take place until January 5, 1949.

Glamorous Glennis is now in the National Air and Space Museum of the Smithsonian Institution, Washington, D.C.

...ovies start? WHEN does a car use overdrive?

WHEN does an atom split?

TALKING MOVIES

The first talking movies were produced in France before 1900 by Léon Gaumont. They were short films, starring great performers such as Sarah Bernhardt, in which the moving pictures were synchronized with a gramophone record. By 1912 Eugene Lauste had discovered the basic method for recording sound on film, while Thomas Edison produced several one-reel talking pictures in the United States. An American, Lee de Forest, improved the system.

In all this the public showed little interest until the presentation on October 6, 1927, of *The Jazz Singer*. This was a silent picture, starring Al Jolson, with four talking and singing interludes. Jolson's electric personality and the very much improved sound began a movie revolution. Within the year every important picture was being produced as a "talkie". By 1930 silent films were a thing of the past, and many film stars found themselves has-beens because their voices recorded badly.

OVERDRIVE

A car uses overdrive when it is travelling at high speed over long distances. Overdrive, or cruising gear, is a device which enables the engine to run at a relatively low speed even when the vehicle is travelling fast.

All internal combustion engines fitted in vehicles need some kind of gearbox because their efficiency at low speeds is poor. The use of different gears enables the speed of the engine to be harmonised with that of the car. The gears may be engaged or shifted by hand or operated by an automatic gearbox.

Most cars have a four-speed gearbox. The driver uses first gear for starting and changes to second and third gears as the car gains speed. Finally in top or fourth gear the engine speed is transmitted unreduced through the gearbox. In overdrive a large gear wheel drives a smaller gear wheel on the propeller shaft. This shaft then rotates faster than the engine, thus reducing wear and tear and saving petrol.

SPLITTING THE ATOM

An atom splits when it is struck by a neutron. The nucleus of the atom then breaks into two roughly equal parts and, at the same time, shoots out several high-speed neutrons.

Atoms are so small that they cannot be seen under the most powerful microscope. They are the building bricks of which each element is composed. The Greek word "atom" means "cannot be cut". But we know now that atoms can be cut, or split. Each one contains minute particles carrying two sorts of electricity: first, the electrons which are negatively charged; and secondly, the central core or nucleus which is made up of protons (positively charged) and neutrons (no charge).

In the 19th Century it was discovered that all elements with atomic weights greater than 83 are radioactive and that the nucleus could be divided into several parts. Albert Einstein (1879–1955) calculated in 1905 that heat ought to have weight and that, if we could destroy a piece of matter and turn all its weight into heat, we should obtain vast amounts of heat by using up only a small amount of matter.

Between 1934 and 1938 the Italian Enrico Fermi and the German Otto Hahn discovered that atoms of uranium (atomic weight 92) split when struck by a neutron. In 1939 Frédéric Joliot-Curie found that this splitting, or fission, released two or three more neutrons which in turn produced fission in more uranium nuclei, and so on. It is this chain reaction that makes possible not only the benefits of nuclear power but also the horrors of nuclear warfare.

Al Jolson appearing in "The Jazz Singer"—the film which delivered the first-ever spoken dialogue—Singer—the film which delivered the first-ever spoken dialogue from the cinema screen—"You ain't heard nothin' yet folks, listen to this."

CONCRETE

Concrete can be said to have been used for thousands of years, if the word is taken generally to mean a hard building material produced from a mixture of cement, sand, gravel and stone. The Assyrians and Babylonians used clay to bind sand and stones, and the ancient Egyptians discovered lime and gypsum. The Romans mixed slaked lime with volcanic ash and constructed aqueducts, bridges and buildings, some of which survive.

Lime remained a popular cementing material until the discovery of the process of making Portland cement shortly after 1800. The name was given to it by Joseph Aspdin, an Englishman, because he thought its products resembled the limestone quarried at Portland in Dorset, England. It is a man-made cement which, since 1900, has been almost the only cement used in the building industry.

Concrete mixtures for small jobs and repairs at home are easily made, but the design and erection of important concrete structures calls for a combination of artistic and scientific skills. Scientists have developed reinforced concrete strengthened with steel, pre-stressed concrete and concrete shells which may be simple and functional or more complex to give a building added beauty.

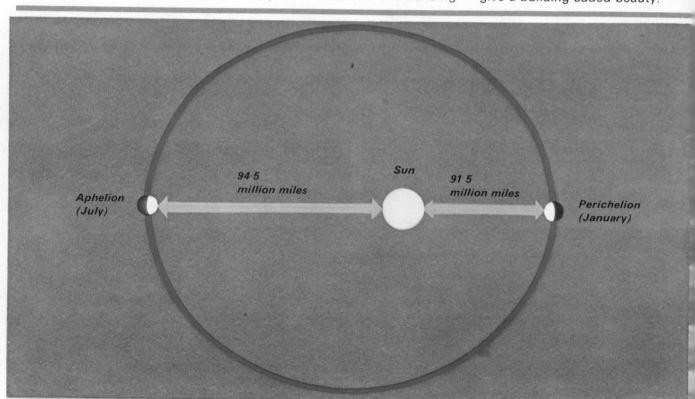

Aphelion (July) — 94·5 million miles — Sun — 91 5 million miles — Perichelion (January)

EARTH AND SUN

The earth is nearest to the sun on about the second or third day in January. The distance varies because the earth spins round the sun in an elliptical orbit or path. The time when the earth is closest to the sun is called the perihelion. The time when it is farthest away—the aphelion—comes six months later on the first or second day in July. During the perihelion the earth is 147 million kilometres from the sun (about $91\frac{1}{2}$ million miles), but during the aphelion it

is 152 million kilometres away ($94\frac{1}{2}$ million miles).

When planetary distances in the solar system are compared, the average distance between these two extremes is used. This is called the astronomical unit and in the case of the earth and sun, measures 149 million kilometres (about 93 million miles). If it were possible for an aircraft to fly from the earth to the sun at a constant speed of 1,000 miles an hour it would have to travel non-stop for

10 years to reach its destination.

The earth takes $365\frac{1}{4}$ days to travel round the sun and moves at a speed of nearly 19 miles a second. As can be seen from the dates of the perihelion and aphelion, the nearness of the sun does not determine the seasons. Our seasons are decided by the amount of daylight and directness of the sun's rays on the earth's surface.

These conditions vary as the axis on which the earth spins is tilted.

o the sun?   **WHEN** was plastic invented?

WHEN does colour fade?

PLASTIC

A plastic, in the modern sense of the word, is a synthetic or man-made material which can be formed into various shapes. The first plastic material was Celluloid, made in 1868 by an American, John W. Hyatt, by dissolving nitrocellulose under pressure.

The use of plastics began slowly, but shortages of natural materials caused by two world wars forced scientists to develop substitutes. Since the Second World War the making of plastics has become a gigantic industry, which has grown so fast that many people still have only a hazy idea what plastics are. In fact, the term "plastics" is as general as the word "metals". The high-temperature cone of a rocket and the highly inflammable table-tennis ball are both plastics, just as lead and steel are both metals.

However, all plastics have some things in common: first, they are entirely man-made and not found in nature; secondly, they consist of large molecules of an organic nature; thirdly, at some stage in their manufacture they are liquid and can be shaped; and fourthly, in their final state they are solid.

Most of the raw materials for plastics are produced by the petroleum and coal industries. Scientists are able to produce different properties in plastics so that they can be used in a tremendous variety of articles.

This giant plastic air-bed makes an ideal playground.

COLOUR FADE

An article's colour fades when subjected to a chemical reaction in which oxygen is released. This oxygen combines with the natural colouring matter or with the dye to produce a colourless compound. Thus the colour of the article becomes paler and is finally taken out altogether, or bleached.

The most famous bleaching agent is the sun, and the process by which it makes colour fade is called photo-chemistry. The old-fashioned method of bleaching textiles by laying them out flat in the sunlight is still used in places.

Chemical bleaching is much quicker, but needs to be controlled with great care. In about 1790 it was discovered that chlorine gas and its compounds were good bleaching agents and chloride of lime (calcium hypochlorite), made by the action of chlorine on slaked lime came into use. This "bleaching powder", as it was called, was dissolved in water. It was removed when the bleaching was complete by washing the article or immersing it in neutralizing solutions. More modern bleaching agents are sodium hypochlorite, hydrogen peroxide and sulphur dioxide.

WHEN does a car engine stall? WHEN does a firestorm

Ruins in Dresden after an incendiary attack.

ENGINE STALL

A car engine will stall—that is to say, it will suddenly stop when you do not want it to—if it is unable to provide sufficient power to overcome the load on the back wheels.

This power is provided by the explosion of the petrol and air mixture pushing down on the pistons. If the load on the pistons from the crankshaft is exerting a greater force than that created by the explosion, the pistons will not move down the cylinder and the engine will stop. This can happen if the clutch is engaged too rapidly or if the hand brake is left on.

FIRESTORM

A firestorm occurs when flames from a large number of individual fires merge into a single convective, or circulatory, column. This produces so much heat that all the buildings below are set on fire. Firestorms cover a whole area, trapping the population within them.

During the Second World War enormous destruction was caused by fire in British, German and Japanese cities. In Britain and Germany the thousands of fires started by incendiary bombs burned individually, with relatively little spread from building to building. This was because of the materials from which the buildings were constructed, their size and the lay-out of the cities.

However, in Japanese cities mostly made up of low wooden-framed houses the American bombing attacks brought about a number of annihilating firestorms. The most terrible of all was that caused by the atomic bomb dropped on Hiroshima, on August 6, 1945. This storm contributed in great measure to the death toll of 70,000 to 80,000 people. In the second atomic bomb attack on Nagasaki on August 9, 1945, fire damage was again severe.

LIGHTHOUSE

The first known lighthouse was the Pharos of Alexandria in Egypt, a 400-foot tower built about 280 B.C. A wood fire was kept burning on the top of the tower, which became one of the Seven Wonders of the World. Before this the light from volcanoes had acted as a guide for sailors. The first lighthouse in Britain was built by the Romans at Dover in about A.D. 43.

Lighthouses continued to be built to the plan of the Pharos until about the 12th Century. Then oil lamps and candles inside lanterns began to be substituted for fires. Shortly afterwards lighthouses suffered a decline which lasted until the great expansion of overseas trade and shipping began in the 16th Century. This led to a revival and many lighthouses were built around the coasts of Europe. The first American lighthouse was constructed on Little Brewster Island off Boston, Massachusetts in 1716.

Electricity was introduced for this purpose by Britain in 1862, when electric carbon arc lamps were installed at Dungeness lighthouse on the coast of Kent. But this source of light did not come into general use until the 1920s, when high-powered filament lamps were employed. A small but powerful high-pressure electric arc lamp containing a gas called xenon was installed at Dungeness in 1961, and mercury arc lamps provide the power for one of the most modern lighthouses in the United States, that on Oak Island, North Carolina.

Scientists are now investigating the possibility of harnessing solar energy to operate lighthouses.

PHAROS

2

WHEN were fireworks introduced? WHEN does a spaceship

FIREWORKS

The use of fireworks, or pyrotechnics, probably began when some prehistoric man mixed saltpetre (potassium nitrate) from his cooking with charcoal from his fire. Saltpetre is a pyrotechnic composition—a substance which does not need oxygen from the air in order to burn, but instead supplies it. Two more such compositions are potassium chlorate and potassium perchlorate. These are combined with finely ground gunpowder, sulphur, aluminium dust and many other chemicals to produce force and sparks, or white or coloured flame. Other substances produce noise, smoke and whistling sounds.

It is believed that fireworks were used in the East, especially China and India, for centuries before they spread to Europe. The Chinese fired pyrotechnic war missiles and produced dazzling displays of fireworks for ceremonial occasions. Arabia, in the 7th Century, also used pyrotechnics in war. In the 14th Century came the invention of gunpowder, a pyrotechnic mixture of saltpetre, charcoal (carbon) and sulphur.

Spectacular firework displays in celebration of victory or peace became popular during the 17th Century. Colour was introduced into the entertainment in the 19th Century through the use of potassium chlorate, which was first prepared by Claude Louis Berthollet (1748–1822). Later magnesium and aluminium was employed to make fireworks still more brilliant. Every year displays are given to mark such widely different occasions as the discovery of the Gunpowder Plot to blow up the British Parliament, and Independence Day celebrations in the United States.

RETRO ROCKET

A spaceship uses a retro rocket when those aboard wish to slow the craft down. The rocket acts as a brake by giving thrust in the opposite direction to the motion of travel. Such a brake is needed to reduce a spaceship's speed sufficiently for it to fall out of orbit and re-enter the earth's atmosphere safely.

A spaceship in orbit travels round the earth at about 17,000 miles an hour. At this speed it has a centrifugal force which counterbalances the inward pull of the earth's gravity, causing it to continue orbiting indefinitely. The problem is overcome by using retro rockets which fire forwards so as to push backwards. This reduces the spaceship's speed and centrifugal force, and allows it to spiral towards the earth. The craft is further slowed down by atmospheric friction and finally by parachutes.

When landing on the moon, where there is no atmosphere, a lunar module is turned round so that its retro rocket is facing the direction of travel. The descent is then controlled by bursts from the retro rocket until just before the module settles on the surface.

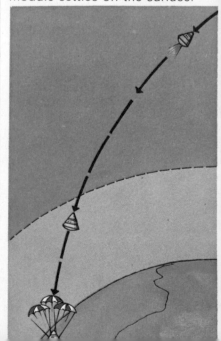

HYDROFOIL

The hydrofoil, a boat supported clear of the water by underwater wings called hydrofoils, was invented by an Italian, Forlanini, in 1898. In 1918 a hydrofoil, powered by an aircraft engine, gained the world's water speed record. The commercial hydrofoils now used in Europe are based on the work of German engineers who carried out research into the design of high-power, lightweight engines.

In the early 1950s hydrofoils were developed in the United States, Canada and Russia using high-powered gas turbines. They are used for both military and commercial purposes.

Since water is 775 times heavier than air, very small hydrofoil wings will support relatively heavy boats. But, since operating in water puts great loads on boats, the hulls are usually built of high-strength steel.

The object in raising the hull of the hydrofoil from the water is to avoid the resistance caused by friction and drag. This means the power needed to drive the boat at high speeds is cut by half. Another result is that the hydrofoil travels smoothly in quite rough water, and is not slowed down.

WHEN were video tapes introduced?   WHEN does a slip

VIDEO TAPES

Video tapes were introduced in the years following the Second World War. The idea of storing information on magnetic wire was first put into practise by a Dane, Valdemar Poulsen, in 1900, but little was heard about it until the 1920s when magnetic tapes were made in the United States and Germany.

The recording of most television programmes is done on magnetic tape or video tape. This technique produces good pictures which can be played back immediately without processing. The magnetic tape, two inches wide, is moved at a speed of 15 inches a second past a magnetic recording head which imprints, by means of electrical signals, a magnetized

pattern of the sound and picture.

The tape is a band of plastic which has a film of magnetic iron oxide coating—one ten-thousandth of an inch thick—spread over one side of it. When the tape is played back, the changing magnetic fields of the pattern of iron oxide particles create weak currents which exactly correspond to the sound and picture which has been recorded.

Recording enables programmes to be re-broadcast or edited. In sports television it is often used for the "instant replay" or reproduction of a particularly interesting event during a live broadcast. Videotape is also employed in slow-motion and stop-action techniques.

SLIP CURRENT

A slip current occurs when a steady stream of air tries to resume its even flow after being diverted by an object at right angles to it. The less streamlined the object, the greater the disturbance; or turbulence, of the stream of air.

A good example is provided by a bus moving along a road. The

IMPLOSION

An implosion is the opposite of an explosion. It occurs when something violently shatters a container in which the internal pressure is less than the external pressure. A good example of such a container is an electric light bulb in which the pressure has been lowered by the withdrawal

GAS BALLOON

The first gas balloon, filled with hydrogen, was released in Paris in August, 1783 by a French professor of physics, J. A. C. Charles. Two months earlier, the first hot air balloon was sent aloft by the Montgolfier brothers, Jacques, Etienne and Joseph, of France, and it was with balloons of this type that the first manned flights were made.

A rubberized silk balloon filled with hydrogen carried Professor Charles and M. N. Robert on a flight of 27 miles and rose to 2,000 feet. Ballooning became a popular sport in spite of the fact that hydrogen-filled balloons were always liable to catch fire. Some amazingly long trips were undertaken, including an unsuccessful attempt in 1958 to cross the Atlantic.

Balloons play an important part in meteorology, the science concerned with the weather. The first aerial photographs were taken from balloons, and in the 1930s pressurized cabins or gondolas were designed enabling observers

to rise over 60,000 feet into the stratosphere.

Military observation balloons fastened to the ground by cables came into use at the end of the 18th Century and were employed by both North and South in the American Civil War (1861–1865). The Austrians used pilotless hot-air balloons to bomb Venice in

1849. During the Franco-German War of 1870–1871 balloons transported mail and carrier pigeons. Barrage balloons tethered to the ground were used in the Second World War to provide barriers against low-flying enemy aircraft.

The Robert brothers help J. A. C. Charles to inflate the first hydrogen balloon.

air pushed aside by the bus is turned back to fill the empty space when the vehicle has passed. Thus air currents are set flowing in the same direction as that being taken by the bus. A sensation of being pulled forward may be felt if you ride a bicycle too close to the rear of a large moving object.

of air. When a bulb is suddenly broken, the atmospheric pressure against all sides causes the glass to collapse inwards with tremendous force and noise.

In contrast, an explosion is caused by a sudden increase of pressure within a confined space, which directs the force outwards.

WHEN does copper turn green? WHEN was the first televisio

GREEN COPPER

Although copper is highly resistant to the chemical action of the atmosphere and of sea water, it turns green if exposed to them for a long time. The colour is caused by the formation of a thin coating of green basic copper carbonate known as patina or verdigris. The latter name comes from the old French *vert de Grece*, (green of Greece), but the reason for it is unknown. This beautiful green is often seen on copper roofs or statues, especially if they are near the sea.

Copper was the first metal man learned to use. Five thousand years ago, when men discovered deposits of pure copper in what are now Iraq and Cyprus, they found that this fairly soft metal could be easily melted, cast in moulds and hammered into tools, weapons and ornaments.

About half the copper produced today is used by the electrical industry. Pure copper is the best cheap conductor of electricity and can be drawn into threads one-thousandth of an inch thick.

ELECTRIC "SHORT"

An electric "short" or short circuit can occur when two wires which are supposed to be separate come into contact, perhaps through loose connections in a socket or worn out insulation. A screwdriver inserted into a socket can also cause a short circuit and severe injury to the person holding it.

Ordinarily the circuit followed by an electric current forces it to overcome certain resistances by generating energy which heats an electric toaster or lights an electric lamp. But when the two sides of an electric circuit are accidentally connected by a path which cuts out this resistance, a short circuit occurs, because electric current always flows through the path of least resistance.

When this happens the current flow becomes so high that it melts the piece of wire or fuse inserted in the circuit as a safety measure and so cuts off the voltage. Damage to an appliance is thereby avoided, for, if the excess current continued to flow, it would cause the appliance to become very hot.

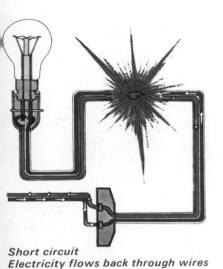

Short circuit
Electricity flows back through wires

TELEVISION

The first public television demonstration or broadcast was given by the British inventor John Logie Baird (1888–1946) in 1926 at the Royal Institution in London. Twenty years earlier Baird had set up a small laboratory at Hastings to study the problem of "seeing by wireless".

Experimental television broadcasts were made by the British Broadcasting Corporation between 1929 and 1935. The pictures were formed of only 30 to 100 lines and flickered badly. It was obvious that a method of high-definition, with more scanning lines, was badly needed.

Research in the United States made possible an increase to 343 lines, and other improvements quickly followed. In November, 1935, the first high-definition television service in the world began with the opening of a B.B.C. station at Alexandra Palace, London, using 405 scanning lines. British television continued with 405 lines until 1964, but now uses the international 625-line standard.

The United States began regular television broadcasting in 1941, but the Second World War held back other countries, and television services did not become

widespread until the 1950s.

Although the first colour television transmission was given by Baird in 1928, its use did not become general until 1954 in the United States, 1960 in Japan and 1967 in Britain, Germany, France, Russia and other countries.

GYROSCOPE

The first gyroscope was made in about 1810 by a German, G. C. Bohnenberger. But the name was the idea of a French physicist, Leon Foucault, in 1852 when he used the device to demonstrate the rotation of the earth. It comes from two Greek words *gyros*, meaning "turn" or "revolution", and *skopein*, meaning "to view". Therefore gyroscope means "to view the turning".

This instrument is based on the principle of a spinning top which remains upright in resistance to the force of gravitation as long as it keeps revolving. In a gyroscope a wheel is mounted in such a manner that it is free to revolve round any axis. When rotating the wheel gives this framework the same tendency to remain at the angle at which it is placed as a top has when it is spinning alone.

Any spinning object resists attempts to change the direction of its axis, the imaginary straight line round which it revolves. Thus you can move a gyroscope up, down, forwards, sideways or backwards and feel no resistance, but you will meet opposition if you try to turn it through an angle.

The gyroscope's other important characteristic is called "precession". This means that when you do overcome the resistance and push the axis out of the straight, the gyroscope does not tilt the way you push it but at right angles to the push and axis.

The peculiar qualities of gyroscopes have been exploited in complex instruments used for stabilizing purposes at sea, on land and in the air. They are used in compasses, gun sights, and instruments for ships and aircraft.

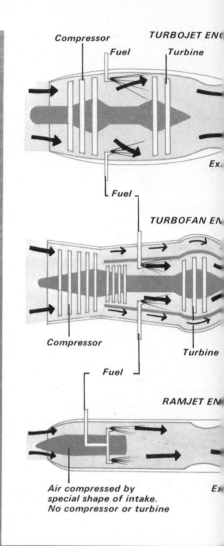

TURBOJET ENG
Compressor
Fuel
Turbine
Ex.
Fuel

TURBOFAN EN
Compressor
Turbine
Fuel

RAMJET EN
Air compressed by special shape of intake. No compressor or turbine
Ex

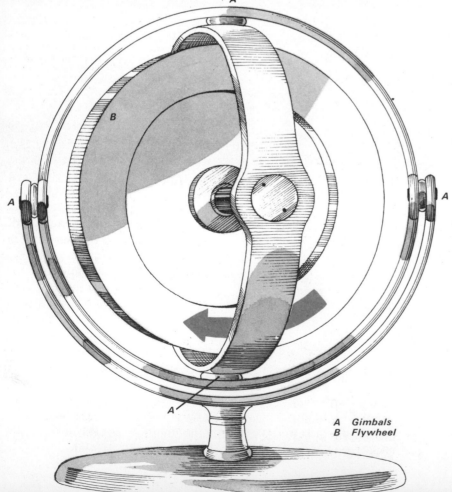

A Gimbals
B Flywheel

SCIENCE

Science began with the wish of some prehistoric man to find out about the workings of the world about him. But the first recorded scientific discoveries are those of the ancient Babylonians who observed the positions of the sun, moon and planets. The ancient Egyptians invented simple arithmetic and geometry around 4,000 B.C. and acquired a considerable knowledge of engineering, medicine and anatomy.

From about 600 B.C. the Greeks made great progress in philosophy and geometry, where intellectual effort only was required. But they achieved little advance in practical science, except for the discoveries of Aristotle (384–322 B.C.), who

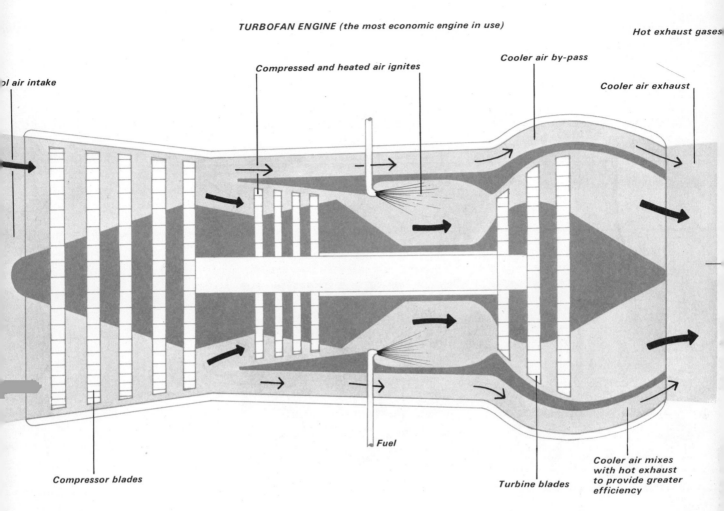

TURBOFAN ENGINE (the most economic engine in use)

Hot exhaust gases

ol air intake

Compressed and heated air ignites

Cooler air by-pass

Cooler air exhaust

Fuel

Compressor blades

Turbine blades

Cooler air mixes with hot exhaust to provide greater efficiency

founded the study of biology. Archimedes (287–212 B.C.) discovered many simple principles of physics and Ptolemy (about A.D. 140) made advances in astronomy.

Under Rome progress slowed down. Then the barbarians overran Europe and for almost 1,000 years—from 300–1100—science was kept alive first in Byzantium and then, from about 700, by the Arabs. From the 15th Century, practical experiments in science began in earnest. Galileo (1564–1642) carried out physical measurements and laboratory experiments. Francis Bacon (1561–1626) and René Descartes (1596–1650) pioneered the new scientific philosophy.

JET ENGINE

The first flight by a jet-propelled aircraft was made in Germany on August 27, 1939. Its engine was designed by Hans-Joachim von Ohain, who had conceived the idea while a student at Göttingen University in Lower Saxony. Unknown to von Ohain, the British inventor and aviator Frank Whittle had thought of the idea some years earlier. But his engine did not have its first flight until May 14, 1941.

Briefly, a jet engine takes in air from the atmosphere, compresses it, and expands it by burning fuel. The mixture of hot gases is then expelled through a nozzle in a powerful backward jet which propels the aircraft forwards.

This forward thrust is the effect of a scientific principle first ex-

plained by the English scientist Sir Isaac Newton (1642–1727). He pointed out that with every action there is a reaction which is equal but opposite to it. Thus when a gun is fired, the forward movement of the shell is matched by the backward recoil of the barrel. In a similar way the reaction to the jet exhaust drives the engine forward. The thrust is obtained by the pressure of the jet against the inside of the nozzle and not, as many people suppose, by the exhaust gases "pushing" against the atmosphere.

The jet engine, whether turbojet, turboprop, ramjet or turbofan, weighs less than a piston engine of comparative power and can be much more streamlined.

General Knowledge

YOGA

Yoga started about the 2nd Century B.C. when its main principles were set forth in the *Yogasutras* by the sage Patanjali. This system of Hindu philosophy is based on the idea that man's bondage results from the identification of the soul with the body and that his freedom comes when he realizes the two can be separated. In yoga the mind is controlled by the constant practise of meditation and non-attachment to material objects.

There are different types of yoga designed for different temperaments. Karma Yoga is suited to active minds, and deals with the performance of duties in which the doer renounces attachment, motive and the result of what he does. Jnana Yoga is for philosophical minds, and teaches how to discriminate between the real and the unreal, and how to renounce the unreal. Bhakti Yoga shows the way to cultivate the love of God for His own sake, deals with self-control and concentration.

The final aim of all these systems is the liberation of the soul from the bondage of matter. Hatha Yoga deals mainly with physical exercises and is chiefly concerned with health and long life. Yoga is a Sanskrit word signifying the union of a person's soul with the supreme spirit. A person who practises yoga is called a yogi.

Two yoga positions. Top: *locust.* Right *variation on the fish.*

SCOUT MOVEMENT

The Scout movement was formed in 1908 after the appearance of a book, *Scouting for Boys*, written by the then Inspector General of Cavalry in the British Army, Lt. Col. Sir Robert Baden Powell. The author had intended his ideas to be used by existing youth organizations, but it soon became evident that a new movement had begun.

Baden Powell had held an experimental camp on Brownsea Island in Poole harbour, Dorset and put into practice his ideas on the training of boys. He thought they should organize themselves into small, natural groups of six or seven under a boy leader. Their training should add another dimension to their education by including mapping, signalling, rope-knotting, first aid and all the skills needed in camping and similar outdoor activities in which self-reliance is important.

Before being accepted as a scout, a boy had to promise to do his duty to God and his country or sovereign, to help other people at all times and to obey the Scout Law. This was a simple code of chivalrous behaviour easily appreciated by boys. It was not long before the movement spread from Britain to other countries.

ALPHABET

The oldest known alphabet was found in Greek inscriptions of about 2000 B.C. The word comes from the first two words of the Greek alphabet, alpha and beta. The alphabet invented in Greece was based on north Semitic writing and was made up entirely of consonants. This was suitable for a Semitic language, but not for a Sudo-European one, such as Greek.

There are two forms of the Greek alphabet called Chalcidic and Ionic and generally known as Western and Eastern. The Western symbols were brought to Italy by Etruscans and Greek colonists, and adapted to form the Latin alphabet used today in most English-speaking, European and American countries.

egin ? **WHEN** was the first alphabet ?

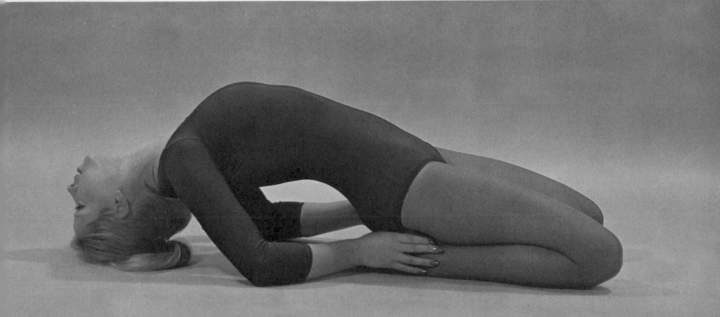

102

WHEN was chess invented? WHEN is food kosher? WHEN

CHESS

Chess was invented in the East, probably by the Hindus in India. In the 6th Century it was introduced to Persia.

But the game of the Hindus and Persians was not the same as modern chess. The Hindus played a four-handed game with four toy armies—elephants, horses, chariots, and foot soldiers. This game was known as *chaturanga* and probably involved the use of dice.

Modern chess, with a chequered board, did not evolve until the 16th Century. Spain and Italy were the first countries to take it up, followed by France and England. The first world chess champion was a Frenchman called Philidor.

KOSHER FOOD

Food is kosher when it has been made fit and clean to eat according to Jewish religious practices.

The food must not come from animals, birds or fish prohibited in the Bibilical books of Leviticus and Deuteronomy.

The meat must be salted to remove the blood after the carcass has been examined for physical defects, and the ischiatic nerve must be removed from the hindquarters, as stated in Genesis.

Meat and milk must not be cooked together and separate utensils must be used.

The *shehita* method of slaughtering is carried out by a specially trained person using a special knife with a smooth, sharp edge. An incision is made across the animal's neck and the knife moved in a fast, uninterrupted sweep without stabbing or pressing. The sweep cuts the main arteries, rendering the animal unconscious and allowing the blood to drip from the body.

was the Identikit invented?

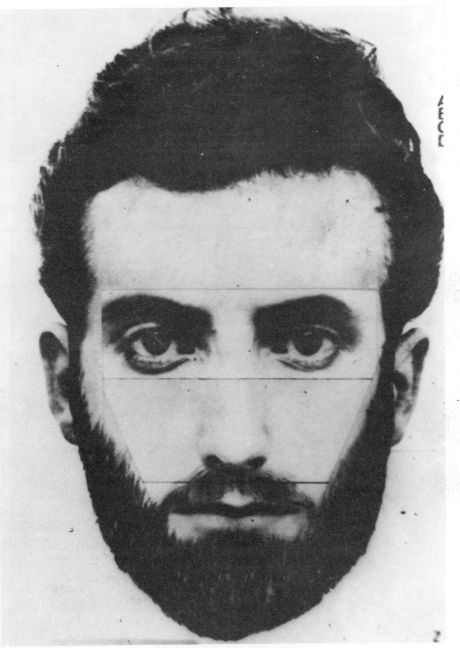

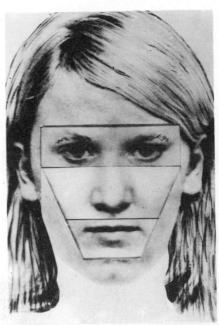

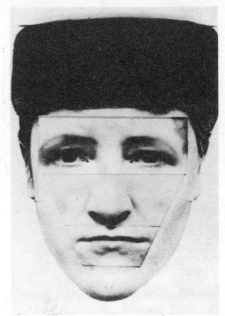

These three pictures have been produced by Photofit.

IDENTIKIT

The Identikit system of building up a picture of someone sought by the police was developed in the United States in 1960 by Hugh Macdonald. It consists of transparent sheets on which are drawn different shapes of faces, eyebrows, noses, mouths and other physical features. These are interchangeable and can be put together according to witnesses' descriptions, thus presenting in one picture their impressions of a wanted person's appearance. A later system called Photofit uses photographs instead of linear drawings.

Both systems are based on ideas similar to those developed in 1879 by Alphonse Bertillon, a French criminologist. Bertillon's system, which was used in many countries until the turn of the century, was founded on three basic principles: that the precise measurements of certain parts of the body can readily be obtained; that these measurements remain constant in a fully grown person; and that no two human beings have exactly the same measurements.

Although most of Bertillon's work involved accurate measurements of the body, an important feature was the *portrait parlé* or descriptive portrait. This was a system of sectional photography introduced to replace the haphazard methods of the time.

JAZZ

The beginning of jazz cannot be dated with accuracy because it is the secular music of the Negro people of the United States and originates in African folk music.

Prominent in the history of jazz is the fundamental flexible music-poetry form called the blues. Here an interplay of African and European musical traditions has produced a flexible folk music of three rhyming lines. One of the great blues singers was Bessie Smith (1894–1937).

Ragtime is very different from the blues, being formal, melodic and fairly limited in rhythm. Its first major composer was Scott Joplin (1868–1917) whose best-known work was *Maple Leaf Rag*.

Between ragtime and orchestral jazz was W. C. Handy, who harmonized blues themes. Then came the New Orleans style, first played by the Original Dixieland Jazz Band in 1917 and best preserved on records by the 1923 group of Joseph "King" Oliver and by "Jelly Roll" Morton's Red Hot Peppers in 1926–1930.

In the late 1920s Louis Armstrong, shown below, emerged as a great solo artist, and in the 1930s and 1940s Duke Ellington's band produced some of the finest jazz. At this time also appeared the Count Basie orchestra, a product of Kansas City and the Southwest. In the next two decades jazz became "cool", with names like Miles Davis and Thelonious Monk. Today, artists like Ornette Coleman are finding new modes of expression in a musical tradition which has its roots in tribal Africa.

CHRISTMAS CARDS

The first Christmas card was designed in England in 1843 by J. C.
Horsley for his friend Sir Henry
Cole. A thousand copies of it were
placed on sale at Felix Summerley's
Home Treasury office in London.
The card was printed by litho-
graphy on stiff dark-brown card-
board and measured $5\frac{1}{8} \times 3\frac{1}{4}$
inches. Underneath the picture of
a family party on the front was the
greeting ''A Merry Christmas and
a·Happy New Year to You''. Inside
were panels, framed in trellis work,
showing examples of Christmas
giving.

Louis Prang of Boston, Massachusetts, is regarded as the ''Father
of the American Christmas card''.
He first produced Christmas cards
in 1875. They were beautifully
designed and much admired
abroad.

SACRED CATS

Cats were regarded as sacred by
the ancient Egyptians 3,000 years
ago. They were worshipped in the
temples and adorned with jewels
in their ears and with necklaces.
Figures of cats were kept in
people's homes and buried in
their tombs.

When cats died they were
buried with great respect amid
public mourning, and their bodies
were mummified to preserve them
for the day of judgment.

Special reverence was paid to
the cat in the temple of Bubastes
where Pasht, the local goddess of
the city, was represented as a
woman with a cat's head. A
festival was held in her honour
every year.

A curious custom which may
have had its origin in pilgrimages
to the goddess's shrine survived
until recent years among Egyptian
Mohammedans. Before starting on
a pilgrimage to Mecca, they would
set apart a camel for the convey-
ance of cats.

BRAILLE

Braille was invented by a Frenchman, Louis Braille, in about 1829. It is an alphabet consisting of an arrangement of raised dots, which can be read by blind people using their sense of touch. While Braille was cutting some leather in his father's shop at the age of three, a knife slipped and plunged into an eye causing blindness.

In 1819, when he was 10 years old, the boy went to Paris with a scholarship to study at the National Institution for Blind Children. The institution's founder hit on the idea of providing texts in embossed Roman lettering which the blind could decipher.

Two years after Braille's arrival Charles Barbier exhibited at the institution an apparatus by which a coded message in dots and dashes could be embossed on cardboard. Braille worked on this system and was able to adapt it to meet the need of the sightless. He published expositions of his system in 1829 and 1837.

Braille became a dedicated teacher at his school and also a talented organist. It was through his life's work that thousands of blind people today can read.

NUCLEAR SUBMARINE

The first voyage under the North Pole was made from August 1 to August 5, 1958, by the United States submarine Nautilus. She crossed from Point Barrow, Alaska to the Greenland Sea, travelling 1,830 miles under the polar ice cap and passing the geographic North Pole on August 3.

The Nautilus could maintain submerged speeds of over 20 knots almost indefinitely.

She was designed to run on direct water heat from an atomic pile. The crew were shielded so well from the pile that in a year's cruise they received less radiation than that set by the American Bureau of Standards as permissible for a single week.

Nuclear submarines are equipped with alternative electrical power for use should the reactor fail.

MAH JONGG

Mah Jongg is probably of 19th Century origin. It is a Western version of a Chinese game and is played with 136 to 144 pieces or tiles, similar to dominoes. These are engraved with Chinese symbols and characters and divided into suits and honours. The object of the four players is to complete combinations or sets of these tiles.

The name Mah Jongg was coined and copyrighted by Joseph P. Babcock, a United States resident of Shanghai, who is credited with introducing the game to the West after the First World War. He wrote a modified set of rules, gave English titles to the tiles and added index letters and numerals familiar to Western card players.

His game became a craze in the United States, Britain and Australia in the mid 1920s. It was revived in 1935 but did not regain its earlier popularity. The words Mah Jongg signify a mythical bird which appears on one of the tiles.

NEWSPAPERS

The earliest regular newspapers of which we have record date back many centuries before the invention of printing to the *Acta Diurna* of the Roman Empire and the gazettes published in China during the first centuries of the Christian era.

The *Acta Diurna* or *Daily Acts* began regular and official publication on the orders of Julius Caesar in 59 B.C. The news was collected by reporters (*actuarii*) employed by the state who posted the *Acta* on a whitened board so that all could read or copy the reports of wars, speeches, legal decisions, political events, marriages, divorces, accidents and deaths.

Pioneers in printing, the Germans were also pioneers in printed newspapers. The first irregular news-sheets began to appear in Cologne, Nürnberg and other cities within 50 years of the invention of modern printing in 1450. By the end of the 17th Century a number of German towns were reading their own daily papers, thus estab-

lishing a tradition for local dailies which has been maintained to this day.

In 1562 Venice had a printed monthly newspaper which was sold for a *gazetta*, a small coin with a name which soon became another word for a newspaper. Among the first journals to use the name was the *Gazette de France* of 1631.

The first regular newspaper in the English language was produced in Holland in 1620 by the English Puritans who later sailed to America in the Mayflower. But more than 80 years were to pass before the first English daily, the *Daily Courant* appeared in 1702.

The first American newspaper, called *Public Occurrences*, was published in Boston on September 25, 1690, but was suppressed by the authorities before it could produce a second issue. The first regular American paper was the Boston *News-Letter* which appeared in April 1704 and ran for more than 70 years.

WHEN was Big Ben built? WHEN was Stonehenge built?

BIG BEN

Big Ben was built in 1858. It is the bell that chimes the hours in the Clock Tower of the British Houses of Parliament, London, and is so called because Sir Benjamin Hall, as the Chief Commissioner of Works, was the minister responsible for its installation. The famous deep, resonant boom of the bell is regularly broadcast by the B.B.C. all over the world.

The way to Big Ben is up a spiral staircase of 374 steps. The Roman numerals on the clock face are two feet high and the pendulum is 13 feet long. Big Ben itself weighs $13\frac{1}{2}$ tons. When the clock was installed, two men used to wind it every week. Now it is wound by electricity.

STONEHENGE

Stonehenge was built on Salisbury Plain, Wiltshire, England, apparently in three different stages between 1800 and 1400 B.C.

The first stage consisted of a circular ditch and bank, with a series of circular holes called Aubrey holes after the man who discovered them. It also included the Hele Stone. There may have been a structure of stone or wood

at the centre of the circle.

During the second stage of construction, which probably took place about 200 years later, the entrance of the earthwork was widened on the east side and connected to the River Avon by a processional way marked by parallel banks and ditches. At the same time a number of Blue Stones, which were apparently brought from the Prescelly Mountains in Pembrokeshire, South Wales, were erected in the centre of the site to form two circles.

The third stage of the work is thought to have been begun after 1600 B.C. The entire monument was remodelled, and about 80 large blocks of sarsen were presumably transported from the Marlborough Downs north of the site. These were erected in a circle of 30 uprights, capped by a continuous ring of stone lintels.

It is generally assumed that Stonehenge was constructed as a place of worship, but its exact purpose is unknown. There is an astronomical explanation for the placing of the stones where they are in relation to the rising and the setting sun.

WHEN was the first steamboat built? WHEN was the first tie
WHEN was the first solo circumnavigation

STEAMBOAT

The first boat ever to be moved by steam power was designed by a Frenchman Jacques Périer and tested on the Seine in Paris in 1775. But the first really successful steamboat was built by Périer's fellow countryman, the Marquis Claude de Jouffroy d'Abbans. His craft which was 141 feet long and equipped with straight-paddled sidewheels travelled several hundred yards against the current on the Saône at Lyons on July 25, 1783.

Among early American pioneers was James Rumsey who in 1786 drove a boat at four miles an hour on the Potomac River, propelled by a jet of water pumped out at the stern. Between 1786 and 1790 John Fitch experimented in the Delaware River at Philadelphia with different methods of propulsion, including paddle wheels, a screw propeller and steam-driven oars.

The first to apply successfully the principle of steam to screw propellers was John Stevens whose boat, equipped with two propellers, crossed the Hudson River in 1804. However, his achievement was soon eclipsed by Robert Fulton's 150-foot long paddlewheeler Clermont which in

This strange steamboat is John Fitch's second boat.

1807 covered the 150 miles from New York to Albany in 30 hours at a maximum speed of five miles an hour. With Fulton in command on the Hudson, Stevens looked elsewhere, and in 1808 his new boat, the Phoenix, sailed out of New York harbour to become the first steamboat ever to go to sea.

Both Stevens and Fulton were

following in the steps of the Scottish inventor William Symington who in 1802 constructed a steamboat in Scotland, the Charlotte Dundas, which was used as a tug on the Forth and Clyde Canal. The Charlotte Dundas was a paddle-wheel steamer. For many years all steamboats used this method of propulsion.

TIE

Today's neckties are the direct descendants of the neckcloths worn by the Croatian troops in the army of the French king Louis XIV (1638–1715). The French called the neckcloth by the same name they called the Croat: *Cravate*. In English it became the cravat, ancestor of the modern tie.

In the mid-1660s men of fashion began to adopt the cravat as a replacement for the large linen collars which were then customary. At first the chosen style consisted of linen strips tied at the throat in a bow with cravat-strings which

were sometimes coloured ribbons. Later the neckcloth was looped at the throat. By the turn of the century it had become wider with tasselled or lace-bordered ends.

Towards the middle of the 18th Century a twist of fashion decreed a stiff, folded neckband called the stock, which fastened at the back of the neck and became higher round the throat as the century progressed. Soon after 1800 the collar of the shirt began to appear above the stock and the neckband was worn almost to the ears.

As collars rose still higher, the

folded stocks gave place to ties. These were sometimes very large, but smaller bow ties with the stocks were quite common. The frilled shirt gave way fast to the plain shirt front visible above the waistcoat. About the year 1840 men about town resorted to turning their collars down.

A Oriental B Mathematical
C Osbaldeston D Napoleon
E American F Mail Coach
G Trone a amour H Irish I Ballroom
J Horse collar K Hunting
L Maharatta M Gordian Knot
N Barrel Knot

vorn?

f the world?   **WHEN** was the Peace Corps started?

CIRCUMNAVIGATION

The first single-handed voyage round the world was achieved by Joshua Slocum in his sloop Spray, between 1895 and 1898.

He wrote about his experiences in his book, *Sailing Alone Around the World*, published in 1900. Slocum was born in Canada in 1844 and died at sea sometime in 1910.

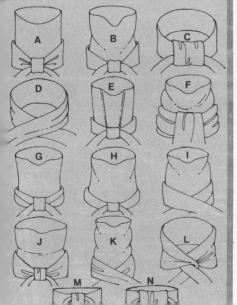

PEACE CORPS

The Peace Corps was established by President John F. Kennedy on March 1, 1961 and became a permanent United States government agency under The Department of State in the following September. Its aim, in the words of President Kennedy, was to create, "a pool of trained American men and women sent overseas by the United States government to help foreign countries meet their need power".

Volunteers for the Peace Corps must be United States citizens and at least 18 years old. An accepted volunteer is assigned to a project requested by a foreign country and prepares for his task by studying for three months at a United States college or university. During this time he learns the language, history, politics and customs of the country to which he is to be sent. When he goes overseas, he works directly with the inhabitants of the country, speaking their language, sharing their lives and receiving a living allowance comparable to that earned by the people among whom he is working.

The normal term of service is two years. In 1961 about 900 volunteers served in 16 different countries of Latin America, Asia and Africa and the number has risen steadily each year. Two years after its foundation the corps won the Ramon Magsaysay Award, the 10,000 dollar prize which is the Asian equivalent to the Nobel Peace Prize. This had never before been won by a non-Asian group.

WHEN is Twelfth Night?   WHEN did Woolworth's begin?

WHEN would a person be excommunicated?
WHEN were traffic lights invented?

TWELFTH NIGHT

Twelfth Night is the night of the twelfth day after Christmas. It is one of the oldest festival days of the Christian Church, and was celebrated as long ago as the 3rd Century. Another name for the festival is Epiphany, or the Feast of the Three Kings. It commemorates the showing of the infant Jesus to the three Magi, or holy men, from the East.

According to tradition Twelfth Night is the day Christmas decorations are taken down.

Detail from Botticelli's Adoration of the Magi.

WOOLWORTH'S

Woolworth's began in 1879 when Frank Winfield Woolworth (1852–1919) opened a "five cent" store in Utica, New York with the financial help of W. H. Moore, a former employer. That store was unsuccessful, but later in the year he opened a "five and ten cent" store in Lancaster, Pennsylvania, with a larger selection of goods to sell. His idea of selling a wide variety of merchandise at two fixed prices proves so popular that he was soon opening stores in other cities.

Similar stores were started by Woolworth's brother, C. S. Woolworth, his cousin, Seymour H. Knox, and his friends, F. M. Kirby and E. P. Charlton. All were merged in 1912 into the F. W. Woolworth company.

When Frank Woolworth died at Glen Cove, Long Island on April 8, 1919, his company owned more than 1,000 stores and his personal fortune amounted to many millions of dollars. The great Woolworth empire still operates and expands throughout the world, and the famous 60-storey Woolworth building in New York, designed by Cass Gilbert in 1931, is regarded as one of the most beautiful early skyscrapers.

EXCOMMUNICATION

Excommunication occurs when a person is punished by being officially excluded from a religious community and banned from entering into "communion" with the other members. The later epistles of St Paul show that this exclusion was carried out as a last resort against those who had "made a shipwreck of their faith", either by immorality or by denying what were regarded as the fundamentals of Christian teaching.

The Roman Catholic Church distinguishes between two types of excommunication, that which leaves a person *toleratus*, or tolerated, and that which makes him *vitandus*, or someone who must be avoided.

Both kinds bar the person from the sacraments of the Church, as well as from Church burial. There is a specific list of offences punishable by excommunication. They include heresy, schism, blasphemous treatment of the eucharist, personal violence against the Pope and membership of forbidden societies.

TRAFFIC LIGHTS

Fixed-time traffic lights were invented in the United States and introduced in New York in 1918. Eight years later the United States set up a Committee on Uniform Traffic Control. The purpose of traffic lights is to control the flow of traffic, determine the right of way at intersections and give greater safety to drivers. By linking successive traffic signals together a progressive movement through the streets can be provided.

Traffic lights were used for the first time in Britain at Wolverhampton, Staffordshire, in 1928. Sixty years earlier the London police had introduced a system of traffic control signals based on the swinging arms of the semaphore.

CIGARETTES

The Spanish conquistadors of 1522 found the Aztec Indians of Mexico smoking a primitive cigarette in the form of tobacco stuffed into a hollow reed or cane tube. Other inhabitants of America at that time crushed shreds of tobacco and wrapped them in corn husks.

However, it was the cigar that the Spaniards brought to Spain as a luxury for the wealthy. The cigarette was improvised early in the 16th Century by the beggars of Seville, who picked up discarded cigar butts, shredded them, rolled them in scraps of paper and called them cigarillos.

It was not until the late 18th Century that they became respectable. The tobacco used for them was of a milder and lighter type, and the French gave them their present name of cigarette or little cigar.

A cigarette factory was set up in Havana in 1853, but the widespread use of the cigarette in the English-speaking world dates from the Crimean War (1854–1856) which introduced British soldiers to Turkish tobacco. Strangely, British taste switched later to straight Virginia tobacco. Americans prefer a blend which includes some of the Turkish variety.

In recent years a connection has been established between cigarette smoking and various diseases of the chest and lungs. There have been many attempts to dissuade the public from smoking and cigarette manufacturers have devoted a great deal of money and research in an attempt to pinpoint and eliminate the harmful elements in tobacco. Filter-tip cigarettes which accounted for only 1·4 per cent of production in 1952, have now risen to more than two-thirds of the total. Many countries have started extensive campaigns to warn of the risks to health.

MARK TWAIN

Mark Twain was the pen-name of the American writer Samuel Langhorne Clemens who was born on November 30, 1835 in the village of Florida, Missouri. He was first apprenticed to a printer and worked on newspapers in New York and Philadelphia. He became apprenticed as a steamboat pilot in 1856 and stayed with the boats until 1861 when he went to Nevada to seek a fortune in mining. In this he was unsuccessful, but he soon obtained a job as a newspaper reporter signing his articles Mark Twain. He took the name from a phrase meaning "two fathoms deep", which he had used to report river soundings during his steamboat career.

The rest of his working life was devoted to writing. He produced books about travel, such as *A Tramp Abroad* and *Roughing It*, but he is best remembered for *Tom Sawyer* (1876) and *The Adventures of Huckleberry Finn* (1884) which tell of the amusing and hair-raising adventures of young boys in the 1830s. The blend of romance, horror and humour in the books has made them favourites with children and adults ever since. Mark Twain was still writing his autobiography when he died on April 21, 1910

ve? **WHEN** was the first pope?

WHEN are people buried at sea?

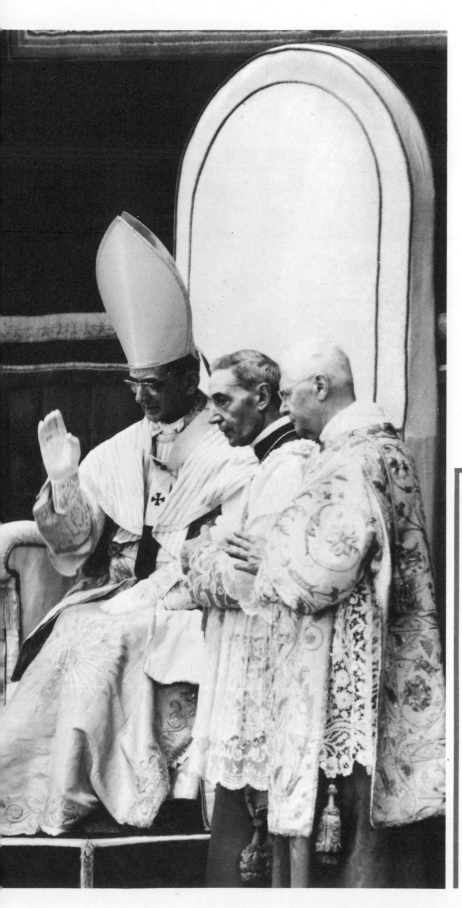

The coronation of Pope Paul VI.

THE POPE

Between the third and fourth centuries, the title of pope was bestowed on bishops other than the head of the Church and sometimes on ordinary priests. The word comes from Latin *papa* (from the Greek *pappas*) meaning father.

The title has been exclusively reserved since the 9th Century for the Bishop of Rome. From the earliest times the Bishop of Rome's claim to the supreme headship of the Roman Catholic Church has been acknowledged by all within the fold. Among his other titles are Holy Father, Vicar of Christ and Pontifex Maximus, meaning chief bridge-builder.

Roman Catholics believe that the Pope is elected as the direct successor of St Peter to be the visible head of the Church on earth. By virtue of his position, he is the Church's supreme governor, judge and teacher.

BURIAL AT SEA

Although burials at sea are much less common than in the days of sailing ships, they still occur on occasions when people die during a voyage and the boat is still a long way from its destination. A service is held on board and the weighted coffin is lowered into the sea.

Sometimes a burial at sea is carried out in accordance with a dead person's wishes, or the ashes are scattered over the waves after a cremation.

In ancient times sea burial was often practised as a cheap method of disposing of dead slaves, foreigners and people considered of little importance. Today some islands, where land is scarce, reserve parts of the sea near the coast as cemeteries.

Viking chiefs before the 10th Century were cremated on burning ships to symbolize a voyage to the land of the dead.

WHEN were keys invented? WHEN did Shakespeare writ

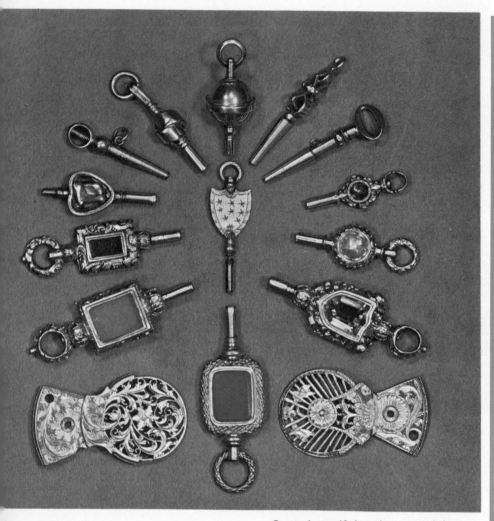

Some beautiful antique watch keys.

KEYS

The first known form of lock and key was used by the Assyrians in the Middle East about 4,000 years ago. This was revealed by the discovery of such a lock in the ruins of the palace of the Assyrian kings at Khorsabad, near the site of the city of Nineveh on the River Tigris in modern Iraq.

The lock was made of wood with the bolt held in a closed position by several loose wooden pins. The lock could be operated by inserting a long wooden key also fitted with pins, which would raise the loose pins enough to allow the bolt to be withdrawn.

This type of lock was apparently known to the Egyptians. It has also been found in Japan, the Faroe Islands and Norway. The long keys were carried on the shoulder, a fact which accounts for the verse in Isaiah 22–22: "And the key of the house of David will I lay upon his shoulder."

Another ancient type of lock known to the Chinese and the ancient Egyptians was the tumbler lock, improved versions of which are still in use today. This lock has small movable levers or "tumblers" and is opened with a key whose indentations will raise each tumbler exactly to the proper height.

Metal locks and keys were invented by the Romans. They designed a lock with a number of ridges or "wards" on the inside. These prevent the turning of the key unless the grooves on it coincide with the wards.

SHAKESPEARE

William Shakespeare (1564–1616), widely regarded as the world's greatest poet and playwright, is believed to have written his 34 plays between 1591 and 1614. His first play is thought to have been *Henry VI* and his last two were probably *The Tempest* and *Henry VIII*.

In 1594 Shakespeare was a member of the Lord Chamberlain's company of players which performed nearly all the time in London. When James I succeeded to the throne in 1603, he took the company under his patronage as the King's Men. They played at the Globe Theatre, Bankside, which was burned down in June 1613 during a performance of *Henry VIII*.

In 1611 Shakespeare left London and lived the life of a retired gentleman in his native Warwickshire town of Stratford-on-Avon.

is plays? **WHEN** was the first home refrigerator?

REFRIGERATOR

The first home refrigerator was made early in the 19th Century in the United States. It consisted of an insulated cabinet into the top of which a block of ice was lowered.

Modern refrigerators which first appeared in 1918 are automatic. They use one of two methods technically known as absorption and compression—to keep foods at temperatures near freezing point, 0° Centigrade (32° Fahrenheit). The period during which foods can be preserved at this temperature is limited to a few days, but in freezers, at temperatures of −18°C (0°F) and lower, they can be stored indefinitely.

The home refrigerator of today is a double-walled box with a hinged door, the space between the walls being filled with insulating material. The door is also double-walled and insulated. A rubber gasket on the inside of the door frame maintains a seal to stop warm air leaking into the box when the door is closed.

bove *Anne Hathaway's cottage where Shakespeare lived in Stratford-on-Avon.* below *The Memorial Theatre at Stratford-on-Avon.*

118

WHEN was the first solo flight across the Atlantic? WHE

SOLO FLIGHT

The first solo flight across the Atlantic was made on May 20–21, 1927, by an American, Charles Lindbergh. He flew from New York to Paris in an aircraft called Spirit of St Louis after the city where the machine was made.

The flight, which took 33½ hours, gained Lindbergh world-wide fame and a prize of 25,000 dollars offered by a man called Raymond Orteig to fly non-stop from New York to Paris. He later made an air tour of the United States, visiting every state and 78 cities.

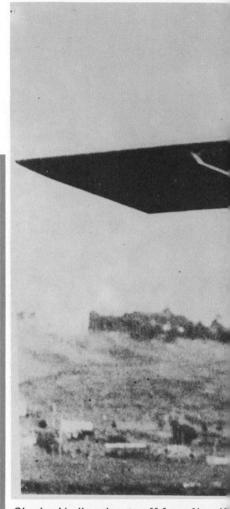

Charles Lindbergh sets off from New Y

REAL ROADS

The earliest artificial roads, as distinct from the natural routes, trails and paths of primitive man, were probably built by the city kingdoms of the Tigris-Euphrates Valley in the Middle East where the first wheeled vehicles may have rolled about 5,000 years ago.

Among the first road engineers mentioned in history were those who accompanied the army of the Assyrian empire-builder Tiglath Pileser I about 1100 B.C. and constructed a route to enable the conqueror to pursue his enemies through the mountains to the north of Mesopotamia. The Assyrians set an example to succeeding empires by establishing an elaborate system of roads for the transport of troops and the dispatch of instructions from the central government to local governors.

Before the coming of the Romans, the biggest and best organized road systems were those belonging to the Persians who founded their empire about 500 B.C., and the rulers of northern India whose dominions around 300 B.C. were already served by a well-equipped highway more than 2,500 miles long. A source of great pride to the Persian Empire, which at one time covered the territory now occupied by Iran, Syria, Iraq, Turkey and northern Egypt, was the so-called Royal Road. This stretched some 1,600 miles from Susa, the capital, to the Aegean Sea, and was provided with staging posts which enabled relays of horses to cover the distance in nine to ten days.

Comparatively few of the roads of antiquity were properly surfaced or metalled until the great Roman engineers began to set a standard for reliability, directness, ingenuity and strength which has not been equalled until recent times. The construction of the Appian Way in 312 B.C. from Rome to the important salt deposits of Capua was the start of a network which provided the empire with vital arteries and gave Europe its principal roads for more than 1,000 years. On the main routes the Romans provided fresh horses at regular intervals to carry imperial messages to and from the capital at speeds of up to 150 miles a day.

Before the Spanish conquests in South America, the great Inca empire, which stretched from Ecuador into modern Chile, was sustained by a 3,200-mile road spanning deep gorges and climbing rocky heights to cross one of the world's most mountainous regions. In North America the first big man-made highway was built in Maryland by a British army on its way to fight the French.

In Europe centuries of neglect were ended with a revival led by two Scottish engineers, John Loudon McAdam (1756–1836) and Thomas Telford (1757–1834). But the world knew nothing to rival the old Roman network until the coming of the automobile produced the 20th Century revolution in overland communications.

vere the first real roads made? WHEN is an overture played?
WHEN is a ruby wedding celebration?

n the "Spirit of St. Louis" on May 20, 1927. Next stop—Europe.

OVERTURE

An overture was originally a piece of music played as an introduction to an opera and suggesting some of the themes that were to follow.

The earliest operas usually opened with a trumpet fanfare or a sung prologue, as in the work of the French composer Luly. This form of the French overture was widely copied by German composers.

A more modern style was established by the German composer Glück who declared that an overture should "prepare the audience for the plot of the play". He meant that the overture should not be brought to a close with the rising of the curtain, but should be merged into the mood of the opening act. Glück's example was followed by Mozart in, for example, his overture to Don Giovanni, and by Beethoven in his overture to Leonore.

Towards the end of the 19th Century the opera overture was frequently replaced by a shorter introductory prelude, notably in Wagner's Lohengrin. This was an entirely new concept which was carried a stage further in Benjamin Britten's overture to Peter Grimes, which consists of only 10 bars.

In the 19th Century the concert overture became established as an independent work, as in the case of Mendelssohn's Hebrides Overture. Some overtures took on the character of symphonic poems.

They are now often heard as part of a concert and not merely as introductions to operas or plays.

RUBY WEDDING

A ruby wedding is celebrated after 40 years of married life. Here are some of the other anniversary celebrations used to mark the passing years of matrimony:

One year, cotton; two years, paper, three, leather; four, silk; five, wood; six, iron; seven, wool; eight, bronze; nine, pottery; 10, tin; 12, linen; 15, crystal; 20, china; 25, silver; 30, pearl or ivory; 35, coral; 40, ruby; 45, sapphire; 50, golden; 55, emerald; 60, diamond; 75, more diamonds.

WHEN was the source of the Nile discovered?

WHEN is Thanksgiving Day

Detail from a portrait of Speke.

NILE SOURCE

The source of the Nile was finally discovered in 1862 by John Hanning Speke when he reached the Ripon Falls at the northern tip of Lake Victoria in Uganda.

Explorers had searched for the spot for centuries. As far back as the 2nd Century the Greek geographer Ptolemy learned enough from travellers' tales to trace a map of the Nile which was later found to be fairly accurate. It was believed that the waters of the Nile came from high snow-covered mountains in central Africa called the Mountains of the Moon.

Modern exploration of the upper part of the Nile began about 1837 when Mohammed Ali, the Turkish ruler of Egypt, ordered a search to be made for the river's source. Three Turkish-led expeditions were made and two of them got to within about 400 miles of their objective.

The Nile runs over 4,100 miles from its source to the Mediterranean.

THANKSGIVING DAY

Thanksgiving Day is an annual national holiday which takes place in the United States and Canada on the last Thursday in November in celebration of the harvest and other blessings during the year.

The first Thanksgiving Day was observed when the Pilgrim Fathers held a three-day festival after the harvest of 1621. But the day was not celebrated as a regular national holiday until more than two centuries later. Gradually each state adopted the idea until, in 1863,

WHEN were the Lyrical Ballads published?

Detail from "The First Thanksgiving", a painting in the Pilgrim Hall Museum.

President Lincoln proclaimed a national harvest festival on November 26.

The festival is still basically a home celebration, with religious overtones, for families and friends. Turkey is the traditional meat at the feast, and such autumnal dishes as pumkin pie and plum pudding stress the harvest theme.

LYRICAL BALLADS

The Lyrical Ballads—one of the most celebrated book of poems ever published in English—were published anonymously in 1798. The ballads were written by William Wordsworth and his friend Samuel Taylor Coleridge and were mainly composed when the two friends lived in Somerset on the slopes of the Quantock Hills. Although very different both in their poetry and in their life styles—Coleridge took drugs and Wordsworth believed in plain living and high thinking—

they shared a common belief that poetry should be simple in form and words and be close to nature. Both sought to break free from the formalities of poetic expression regarded as "tasteful" at that time.

Coleridge's chief contribution to the Ballads was The Ancient Mariner. Wordsworth's preface to the book expounded his new principles of poetry. Although the book created little interest when it first appeared, it is now recognised as a turning point in English poetry.

ROUND EARTH

Greek scholars had decided by 350 B.C. that the earth must be round. But the earlier belief that it was flat persisted in other countries for many centuries afterwards. Even as late as the time of Christopher Columbus, at the end of the 15th Century, a fear of falling off the edge of the earth existed among seamen.

One theory held by early man was that the sky was a kind of shield which came down to meet the earth on all sides, forming a boxed-in universe. It was the Greeks who hit on the idea that it was a circular slab. A Hindu myth suggested that the slab was supported by four pillars which rested on four elephants, which stood on a gigantic turtle, which, perhaps, swam in a huge ocean.

The Greek philosopher, Anaximander of Miletus (611–546 B.C.) thought man might be living on the surface of a cylinder, which was curved from north to south. He was the first, as far as is known, to suggest any shape for the earth other than that it was flat.

BEAUTY SPOTS

The first women on record as having worn beauty spots on their faces were leaders of fashion in the days of the Roman Empire. These spots were small and round, and evidently worn in great profusion. The poets Ovid (43 B.C.–A.D. 18) and Martial (about A.D. 40–104) were among the classical writers to comment on the habit.

Beauty spots then seem to have gone out of fashion until they reappeared late in the 16th Century. Their return is believed to have started with the use of black velvet or taffeta court-plasters on the temples for the relief of toothache. Women found them more effective in improving their complexion by setting off the whiteness of the skin.

The patches were usually placed near the mouth. As the craze for them developed they became much bigger and were cut to different shapes and patterns.

In London, beauty spots took on political significance. Supporters of the Whig party wore them on the right cheek, those of the Tory party on the left. In 1711 a writer in *The Spectator*, a famous London magazine, noted that women "would be more beautiful than the sun were it not for the little black spots that break out and sometimes rise in very odd figures. I have observed that these little blemishes wear off very soon but, when they disappear in one part of the face, they are very apt to break out in another. I have seen a spot in the forehead in the afternoon which was upon the chin in the morning."

In Paris the fashion produced elaborate variations. One marquise is reported to have appeared at a party wearing 16 patches in the shape of a tree in which perched two love birds. Men also adopted the vogue.

These "little blemishes", cut out of silk, taffeta, velvet and even leather, and stuck on with mastic, continued to wander about the faces of women until the middle of the 19th Century.

A strange assortment of patches worn in the time of Charles I of England. From Fairholt's "Costume in England".

ealize that the earth is round?

ouse? **WHEN** is eating meat forbidden to certain people?

EXORCISM

A service of exorcising a house is sometimes carried out by a priest when the building is said to be haunted by a spirit. The ceremony involves the performance of a set ritual and, in some cases, the sprinkling of holy water.

The photograph shows the ruins of Borley Rectory near Chelmsford, in Essex, Elgnald. This was once said to be the most haunted house in England and it still has an awesome reputation.

EATING MEAT

Some religions forbid their followers to eat certain kinds of meat. Under the rules for kosher food, Jews must not eat the flesh of pigs and other animals prohibited in the biblical books of Leviticus and Deuteronomy. Hindus are not permitted to eat beef because, in their religion, the cow is a sacred animal. The ancient Celts worshipped Epona, the horse goddess, and were, therefore, not allowed to eat horse flesh.

Until recently Roman Catholics were not supposed to eat meat on Fridays as a gesture of self-sacrifice on the day of the Crucifixion. Fish was substituted. Nowadays some other gesture is often made, such as giving money to charity.

Vegetarians are people who do not eat meat, either for health reasons or on humanitarian grounds, believing that it is wrong to kill animals for food.

DAY OF JUDGMENT

A vivid picture of the Day of Judgment is drawn in the New Testament book of Revelation. The Bible tells us that at some time not yet revealed the end of the world will come and there will be a Universal Day of Judgment. On that day all people will be called from the dead to face the judgment of God.

The Christian Church however has another interpretation of the Day of Judgment as the day of our death. On that day, according to this interpretation, we have to expect to meet our Creator and answer for our sins.

Detail from The Triumph of Death by Peter Breughel the Elder.

BALLPOINT PEN

The first workable ballpoint pen was patented in 1937 by Laszlo Jozsef Biro, a Hungarian living in Argentina, but ideas for ballpoint pens date back to the late 1890s. Biro's pen became popular during 1938 and 1939.

The United States forces welcomed it because the Quartermaster General of the Army had called for a writing instrument which would not leak at high altitudes, would use a quick-drying ink unaffected by changes in climate and would contain enough ink to last for a considerable time.

In this type of pen a ball, housed in a socket at the tip, transfers special ink from a reservoir on to the surface of the writing paper. The inks used have dyes which are soluble in oil or spirit. The first type dries because it is absorbed into the paper, the second because it evaporates.

At one time most of the balls used in high-quality ballpoint pens. Most manufacturers use a ball one millimetre in diameter.

en first come into use?

WHEN were wigs first worn? WHEN was ice cream invented

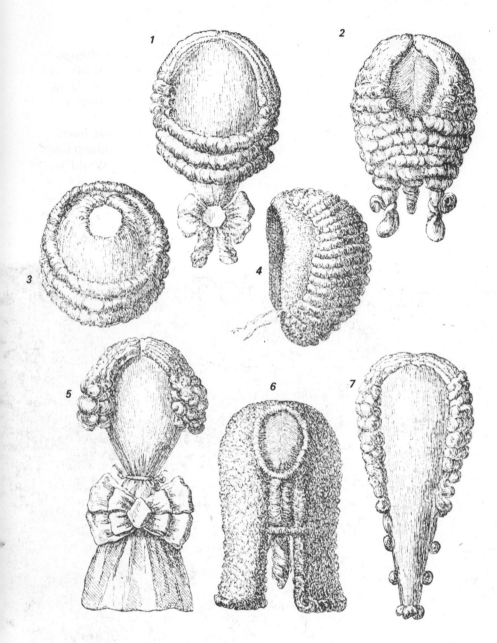

1 Wig a la brigadie 2 Knotted wig 3 Abbe's wig 4 Woman's wig 5 Bag-wig
6 Square-wig 7 Newly growing wig

WIGS

The wearing of wigs by both men and women dates from our earliest recorded history. Wigs have been found on Egyptian mummies, and the appearance of the frizzled-out hair on some of the figures on the frescoes at Knossos suggests that wigs were also familiar to the ancient civilization of Crete. The Medes and Persians also wore artificial hair, and Greek women were using hairpieces by the 4th Century B.C. The Romans began wearing wigs in the early years of the Empire.

The word wig is a shortened version of periwig, which is derived from the French perruque. It was in 17th-Century France that wigs began to assume their greatest glory as features of men's fashion. Louis XIV, who was very proud of his own hair when he was young, did not wear a wig until after 1670 when he was in his 40s. From Versailles, the fashion then spread throughout Europe.

During the first decade of the 18th Century men's wigs reached their maximum size, covering shoulders and back, and floating down over the chest. After that they gradually became smaller until, for normal wear, they disappeared. In recent years wigs have again become popular with women and the wearing of artificial hairpieces has become an accepted device among men.

ICE CREAM

Water ices were known in the Roman Empire, and Marco Polo (1254–1324) is said to have brought back a recipe for milk ices from his travels in the Far East.

Centuries later, chefs for the royal courts of Europe were experimenting with ice cream and trying, without success, to keep the recipes secret. In the 19th Century the commercial production of ice cream was made possible by the discovery that ice mixed with salt produced a lower temperature than ice alone. The industry grew rapidly towards the end of the century because of the introduction of mechanical refrigeration.

About 80 per cent of the liquid mixture for making ice cream is milk and cream, and about 15 per cent is sweetener. Sometimes egg yolk is also used, and fruit, nuts and flavourings are often added to the mixture.

Most commercial ice cream is made in a refrigerated tube with revolving blades or beaters. The partially frozen ice cream is drawn off into containers and sent to a hardening room with a temperature of from −18° to −26° Centigrade (0° to −15° Fahrenheit). It is then delivered in refrigerated trucks to dealers. Strict standards of hygiene have to be maintained.

WHEN was silk first used in Europe?

SILK IN EUROPE

Rome began to import raw silk from the East towards the beginning of the Christian era. When silk first appeared in Europe it was enormously expensive—literally worth its weight in gold—and its use by men was considered effeminate.

The industry of silk weaving began in ancient China. By the 2nd Century, silk weaving flourished in Egypt, Syria and Palestine. By the 4th Century the industry had spread to Constantinople, and Byzantine silks became world famous. When the Moors captured Sicily in the 11th Century, the established silk weaving there. After the Norman conquest of Siciliy in the 11th Century, the industry spread to the cities of Florence, Genoa, Milan and Venice.

Silkworms were introduced to the New World in 1522, by Hernán Cortés in Mexico, but the experiment failed. Since then sericulture, or the making of silk, has been introduced in the United States, but has never become a major industry.

In spite of the progress made in man-made fibres for clothing since the end of the Second World War, silk remains a first choice for luxurious and expensive clothes because of its delicacy, relative strength, elasticity and ability to take colour.

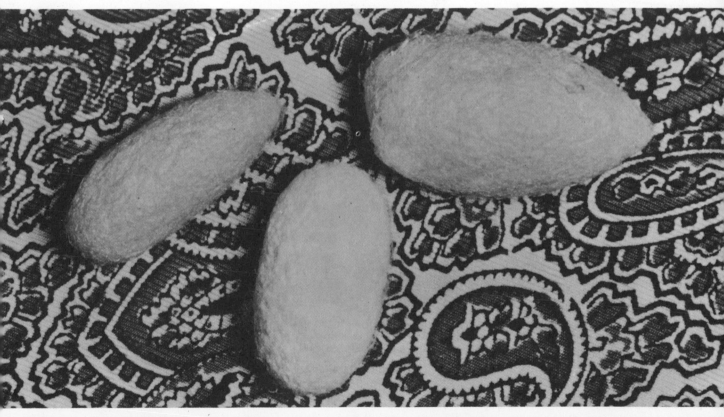

ACKNOWLEDGEMENTS

The publishers would like to thank the following organizations and individuals for their kind permission to reproduce the pictures in this book:

Ardea 12 (I. R. Beaches). 17 (Kenneth Fink)

BBC 94

BPC/Phoebus Picture Library 121

Barnaby's Pjcture Library 23 left (Richard Backlund). 32/33, 54, 3 bottom right and 75 bottom right, 77, 80, 81 bottom left, 84, 101 top, 108, 119, 123

Bodleian Library, Oxford 45

Bulloz, Paris 49

Camera Press 37 all, 43, 52, 53 top right, 53 bottom left, 62 centre right, 79

Bruce Coleman 1, 8 top right (G. J. Deans), 9 (Jane Burton), 16 (Jane Burton), 20 (Allan Power), 25 top right, 56 bottom left, 56 bottom right (M. F. Soper)

Colour Library International 68, 73, 81 top centre

Cooper-Bridgeman 39, 112

Cinema Bookshop 87

Mary Evans Picture Library 2 bottom right, 19, 26, 27, 31, 38, 122 top left, 122 top right, 126

Flight Magazine 2 bottom left, 86

Michael Holford 28, 29, 30, 40, 48, 105, 120, 124/125

Keystone 55, 59, 66, 70, 74, 75 top left, 89, 90, 103, 104, 106, 107, 111 bottom right

Frank Lane 2 top right, 8 bottom left (Laurence Perkins), 14, 15 top left, 15 bottom right, 76 bottom right (F. Lane)

Mansell Collection 34, 35, 36, 44, 82, 91, 102, 110, 111 top right, 114

NHPA 10 (S. Dalton), 21 top centre (S. Dalton), 22 (S. Dalton), 24 (Brian Hawkes), 62 centre left, 127 middle centre (S. Dalton), 127 bottom centre (S. Dalton)

Picturepoint 13 top centre, 13 bottom right, 69, 72, 76 top left, 81 bottom right, 85 top, 93, 109, 117 top left, 116 top left, 116 top right

Popperfoto 3 top, 11 top left, 111 bottom left, 42, 46

Radio Times Hulton Picture Library 63, 97

Rex Features 118

Ronan Picture Library 67, 83, 95

The Scout Association 100

Spectrum 85 bottom left, 92, 96, 117 bottom centre

Tourist Photo Library 41

Illustrations by Ben and Stephanie Manchipp